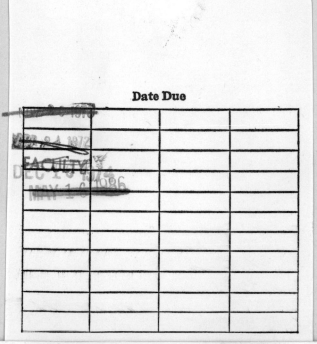

Date Due

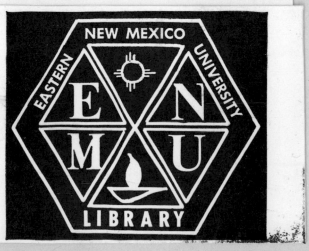

GEORGE BERNARD SHAW

THE PERFECT
WAGNERITE

*A Commentary on the
Niblung's Ring*

DOVER PUBLICATIONS, INC.
NEW YORK

This Dover edition, first published in 1967, is an unabridged and unaltered republication of the fourth edition (1923), as published by Constable & Co., London.

Library of Congress Catalog Card Number: 66-29055

Manufactured in the United States of America
Dover Publications, Inc.
180 Varick Street
New York, N. Y. 10014

CONTENTS

PREFACE TO THE FOURTH EDITION

Much water, some of it deeply stained with blood, has passed under the bridges since this book was first published twenty-four years ago. Musically Wagner is now more old-fashioned than Handel and Bach, Mozart and Beethoven, whose fashions have perished though their music remains; whilst his own fashion has been worn to rags by young composers in their first efforts to draw the bow of Ulysses. Finally, it has been discarded as Homerically impossible; and England, after two centuries of imitative negligibility, has suddenly flung into the field a cohort of composers whose methods have made a technical revolution in musical composition so complete that the conductor does not dare to correct the most cacophonous errors in band parts lest the composer should have intended them, and looks in vain for key signatures because young men no longer write in keys but just mark their notes flat or sharp as they come. One can imagine Wagner trying to conduct the latest British tone poem, and exclaiming in desperation, "Is this music?" just as his own contemporaries did when they were confronted with the "false relations" in the score of *Tristan*. It is true that most of the modern developments, as far as they are really developments and not merely experimental eccentricities, are implicit in *Parsifal*. Indeed, for that

matter, they are implicit in Bach: still, the first man to be
scandalized by a new departure is usually he that found the
path for it; and I cannot feel sure that Wagner would have
encouraged Messrs. Bax, Ireland, Cyril Scott, Holst,
Goossens, Vaughan Williams, Frank Bridge, Boughton,
Holbrooke, Howells and the rest (imagine being able to
remember off hand so many names of British composers turning out serious music in native styles of their own! ! !) any
more than Haydn encouraged Beethoven. Wagner, after
his 1855 London season as conductor of the Philharmonic,
would not have believed that such a thing could happen in
England. Had he been told that within two years a British
baby Elgar would arrive who would attain classic rank as a
European composer, he would hardly have kept his temper.
Yet all this has happened very much as it happened before
in Shakespeare's time; and the English people at large are
just as unconcerned about it, and indeed unconscious of it, as
they were then.

Also the English have taken, as I said in this book they
might, to Wagner singing and acting; and there is now no
question of going to Bayreuth or importing German singers
when we wish to hear *The Ring* or *Parsifal*; for much better
performances of both can be heard now from English
companies in England than Wagner ever heard at Bayreuth;
and even a transpontine theatre like the Old Vic. thinks no
more of doing *Tannhäuser* than it would have thought of
doing *Black-Eyed Susan* half a century ago.

Another change has outmoded my description of the
Bayreuth Festival Playhouse as an ultra modern theatre.
Bayreuth has a pictorial stage framed by a proscenium, and
the framed picture stage is not now in the latest fashion.
When the monarchy and the theatre were restored in
England simultaneously on the accession of Charles II, the
representation of Shakespeare's plays as he planned them
was made impossible by the introduction of pictorial

scenery and of the proscenium with its two curtains, the act drop and the final green baize, to divide the plays into acts and hide the stage for intervals during which elaborate scenes were built up on it. His plays had to be chopped into fragments; divided into acts; rewritten and provided with new endings to make effective "curtains," in which condition they were intolerably tedious except as mere pedestals for irresistibly attractive actors and actresses.

Thus the pictorial stage not only murdered Shakespeare, and buried the old Athenian drama, but dictated the form of opera (which grew up with it) and changed the form of the spoken drama. Wagner submitted to it as inevitable; but when he conceived the performances of *The Ring*, and planned a theatre for them, he made a desperate effort to elaborate its machinery so as to enable complete changes of scene to be made without stopping the performance and keeping the audience staring idly for fifteen minutes at a dropped curtain, or scrambling to and from their seats to fill up the time by smoking cigarets and drinking. One of his devices was to envelop the stage in mists produced by what was called a steam curtain, which looked exactly like what it really was, and made the theatre smell like a laundry. By its aid *The Rhine Gold* was performed without a break instead of in three acts with long intervals between each.

One had to admit at Bayreuth that here was the utmost perfection of the pictorial stage, and that its machinery could go no further. Nevertheless, having seen it at its best, fresh from Wagner's own influence, I must also admit that my favorite way of enjoying a performance of *The Ring* is to sit at the back of a box, comfortable on two chairs, feet up, and listen without looking. The truth is, a man whose imagination cannot serve him better than the most costly devices of the imitative scenepainter, should not go to the theatre, and as a matter of fact does not. In planning his

Bayreuth theatre, Wagner was elaborating what he had better have scrapped altogether.

But as this did not occur to him, he allowed his technical plan of *The Ring* to be so governed by pictorial visions that it is as unreasonable to ask Bayreuth to scrap the Wagner tradition as it would be to ask the Théâtre Français to scrap the Molière tradition. Only, I must now treat that tradition as old-fashioned, whereas when this book was first published it was the latest development. What has happened since in England is that an Englishman, Mr. Harley Granville-Barker, developing certain experiments made from time to time by Mr. William Poel, another Englishman, inaugurated twentieth century Shakespeare by a series of performances in which the plays were given with unprecedented artistic splendor without the omission of a single decently presentable line, undivided into acts, without the old pictorial scenery, and with, as a result, a blessed revelation of Shakespeare as the Prince of Entertainers instead of the most dreaded of bores, and a degree of illusion which the pictorial theatre had not only failed to attain, but had sedulously destroyed, nowhere more effectively than (save only in certain scenes of pure ritual in *Parsifal*) at Bayreuth.

Almost simultaneously with Mr. Granville-Barker's revolutionary restoration of Shakespeare, the pictorial stage triumphantly announced that at the English Bayreuth, which is the Shakespeare Memorial Theatre at Stratford-on-Avon, the play of *Coriolanus* had been, by a climax of Procrustean adaptation, cut down to a performance lasting only one hour, in which state it was humbly hoped that the public would steel itself to bear it just once or twice for the sake of our national playwright. That was too much. Mr. Bridges Adams, who had started with Mr. Granville-Barker, took the new method to Stratford, where the former victims of the pictorial stage now find to their amazement that three hours of unabbreviated Shakespeare fly faster than one hour of Procrusty *Coriolanus*. And at the Old Vic. in London, where the reform was adopted by Mr. Atkins, Shakespeare now draws better than would-be popular melodrama.

Thus have Englishmen left Wagner behind as to methods, and made obsolete all that part of this book which presents him as a pioneer. I must add that nobody who knows the snobbish contempt in which most Englishmen hold one another will be surprised when I mention that in England the exploits of Poel, Granville-Barker, Bridges Adams, Atkins, and the English designers and painters who have worked for them, are modestly attributed to Herr Reinhardt, their eminent German contemporary. The only Englishman who is given any credit by his countrymen is Mr. Gordon Craig, a fascinating propagandist who still loves the stage picture better than the stage play, and, living in the glamor of the Continent, seldom meddles with the actual theatre except to wipe his boots on it and on all the art that grows on its boards.

As to the sociological aspect of *The Ring*, which is unaffected by the rapid ageing of its technical aspect as a musical composition and a theatrical spectacle, it seems to challenge the so-called Great War to invalidate it if it can. Gross as the catastrophe has been, it has not shaken Bayreuth. But post-war contemplation of *The Ring* must not make us forget that all the progress Wagner saw was from the revolutions of 1848, when he was with the barricaders, to the Imperialist climax of 1871, when he sang:

> Hail, hail, our Cæsar!
> Royal William!
> Rock and ward of German freedom!

What would he have said had he lived to see 1917 in Russia and 1918 in Germany, with England singing "Hang, hang that Kaiser!" and Germany sympathizing to such an extent that the grandson of Wagner's William had to seek safety in Holland. Rhinemaidens walking out with British Tommies, Senegalese negroes in Goethe's house, Marx enthroned in Russia, pistolled Romanoffs, fugitive Hapsburgs, exiled Hohenzollerns marking the ruins of empires with no more chance of restoration than the Stuarts and Bourbons: such a Götterdämmerung, in short, as in its craziness can be fitted into no allegory until its upshot becomes plainer than it now is: all this has so changed the political atmosphere in which Wagner lived, and in which this book was written, that it says much for the comprehensiveness of his grasp of things that his allegory should still be valid and important.   Indeed, the war was more a great tearing off of masks than a change of face: the main difference is that Alberic is richer, and his slaves hungrier and harder worked when they are so lucky as to have any work to do.   *The Ring* ends with everybody dead except three mermaids; and though the war went far enough in that conclusive direction to suggest that the next war may possibly kill even the mermaids with "depth charges," the curtain is not yet down on our drama, and we have to carry on as best we can.   If we succeed, this book may have to pass into yet another edition: if not, the world itself will have to be reedited.

Ayot St. Lawrence, 1922.   G. B. S.

PREFACE TO THE THIRD EDITION

In 1907 *The Perfect Wagnerite* was translated into German by my friend Siegfried Trebitsch. On reading through his version in manuscript I was struck by the inadequacy of the merely negative explanation given by me of the irrelevance of *Night Falls on the Gods* (*Die Götterdämmerung*) to the general philosophic scheme of *The Ring*. That explanation was correct as far as it went; but, put as I had put it, it seemed to me to suggest that the operatic character of *Night Falls on the Gods* was the result of indifference or forgetfulness produced by the lapse of twenty-five years between the first projection of *The Ring* and its completion. Now it is clear that in whatever other ways Wagner may have changed, he never became careless and never became indifferent. I therefore inserted in the first German edition a new section in which I shewed how the revolutionary history of Western Europe from the Liberal explosion of 1848 to the confused attempt at a popular and *quasi* Socialist military and municipal administration by the Commune of Paris in 1871 (that is to say, from the literary beginning of *The Niblung's Ring* by Wagner to the long-delayed musical completion of *Night Falls on the Gods*) had demonstrated practically that the passing away of the present capitalistic order was going to be a much more complicated business than it appears in Wagner's dramatization.

Since 1907, then, the German edition has been more complete than the English one. I now, after six years' pure procrastination, for which I have no excuse except pre-occupation with other work, add the German extension to the English text. It begins on page 87, and ends on page 94. Otherwise the book remains as it was.

I have sometimes been asked why anyone should read a philosophic treatise merely to find out the story of *The Ring*. I take this opportunity to reply publicly that there is, as far as I know, no reason why anyone should take any trouble in the matter at all unless they want to, and that the degree of trouble must be determined by the degree of.want, which, again, will be determined by the wanter's capacity. But this I will say. Even for the purposes of the idlest Bayreuth tourist the story of *The Ring* must be told as Wagner's score tells it if it is to be of any real use to the visitor who cannot understand what the singers are saying. Anyone can, without knowing a bar of the score, string the events narrated in *The Ring* together in the order of their occurrence on the stage, add the names of the *dramatis personæ* and a description of the scenes, and offer the result as a guide to *The Ring*. But such a mechanical account of the affair will hinder more than it will help. It will pass over as trivial, or even omit altogether, points to which Wagner has given immense weight and consequence, either by the length or intensity of his direct musical treatment or by the recurrence of themes connected with them; and it will rhetorically emphasize or spread itself descriptively over the more obvious matters which speak for themselves to the spectator and occupy little space and less depth in the musical fabric. People primed with such accounts sit waiting to see the bear or the dragon or the rainbow, or the transformation of Alberic into a snake and a toad, or the magic fire or the swimming feats of the Rhine daughters, and are bored because these exciting spectacles are so unconscionably delayed whilst Wotan, Fricka, Brynhild, Erda, Alberic and Loki discuss things of which the "synopsis" gives no hint.

Now the story as it is told in this book has its centres of gravity placed exactly where Wagner has placed them in his score. What Wagner has made much of, I have made much of; and I have explained why he made much of it. What he passed lightly over, I have passed lightly over. There is a good deal in *The Ring* which is on the surface of the score: nobody with ears and eyes can miss its significance at the performance. But there is also a good deal that was at the back of Wagner's mind, and that determined what I have called the centres of gravity; and this, which is neither in the score nor in the stage action, being assumed by Wagner to be part of the common consciousness of mankind, is what I have chiefly attended to. For this, obvious as it was to Wagner, and as it is to anyone who has reflected on human history and destiny in the light of a competent knowledge of modern capitalistic civilization, is an absolute blank to many persons who are highly susceptible to the musical qualities of Wagner's music and poetry, but have never reflected on human destiny at all, and have been brought up in polite ignorance of the infernal depths our human society descended to in the nineteenth century. Clearly none of your synopses or popular guides or lists of musical themes would be of the slightest use here. That, I take it, is why this little book remains, after some fifteen years, still in demand, and why I have found it necessary to complete it in this edition by a chapter dealing neither with music nor poetry, but with European history. For it was in that massive material, and not in mere crotchets and quavers, that Wagner found the stuff for his masterpiece.

Ayot St. Lawrence, 1913.   G. B. S.

PREFACE TO THE
SECOND EDITION

The preparation of a Second Edition of this booklet is quite the most unexpected literary task that has ever been set me. When it first appeared I was ungrateful enough to remonstrate with its publisher for printing, as I thought, more copies than the most sanguine Wagnerite could ever hope to sell. But the result proved that exactly one person buys a copy on every day in the year, including Sundays; and so, in the process of the suns, a reprint has become necessary.

Save a few verbal slips of no importance, I have found nothing to alter in this edition. As usual, the only protests the book has elicited are protests, not against the opinions it expresses, but against the facts it records. There are people who cannot bear to be told that their hero was associated with a famous Anarchist in a rebellion; that he was proclaimed as "wanted" by the police; that he wrote revolutionary pamphlets; and that his picture of Niblunghome under the reign of Alberic is a poetic vision of unregulated industrial capitalism as it was made known in Germany in the middle of the nineteenth century by Engels' *The Condition of the Working Class in England in 1844*. They frantically deny these facts, and then declare that I have connected them with Wagner in a paroxysm of senseless perversity. I am sorry I have hurt them; and I appeal to charitable publishers to bring out a new life of Wagner, which shall describe him as a court musician of unquestioned fashion and orthodoxy, and a pillar of the most exclusive Dresden circles.   Such a work, would, I believe, have a large sale, and be read with satisfaction and reassurance by many lovers of Wagner's music.

As to my much demurred-to relegation of *Night Falls on the Gods* to the category of grand opera, I have nothing to add or withdraw.   Such a classification is to me as much a matter of fact as the Dresden rising or the police proclamation; but I shall not pretend that it is a matter of such fact as everybody's judgment can grapple with.   People who prefer grand opera to serious music-drama naturally resent my placing a very grand opera below a very serious music-drama. The ordinary lover of Shakespeare would equally demur to my placing his popular catchpenny plays, of which *As You Like It* is an avowed type, below true Shakespearean plays like *Measure for Measure*.   I cannot help that.   Popular dramas and operas may have overwhelming merits as enchanting make-believes; but a poet's sincerest vision of the world must always take precedence of his prettiest fool's paradise.

As many English Wagnerites seem to be still under the impression that Wagner composed *Rienzi* in his youth, *Tannhäuser* and *Lohengrin* in his middle age, and *The Ring* in his later years, may I again remind them that *The Ring* was the result of a political convulsion which occurred when Wagner was only thirty-six, and that the poem was completed when he was forty, with thirty more years of work before him.   It is as much a first essay in political philosophy as *Die Feen* is a first essay in romantic opera.   The attempt to recover its spirit twenty years later, when the music of *Night Falls on the Gods* was added, was an attempt to revive the barricades of Dresden in the Temple of the Grail. Only those who have never had any political enthusiasms to survive can believe that such an attempt could succeed.

London, 1901.   G. B. S.

PREFACE TO THE
FIRST EDITION

This book is a commentary on *The Niblung's Ring*, Richard Wagner's chief work. I offer it to those enthusiastic admirers of Wagner who are unable to follow his ideas, and do not in the least understand the dilemma of Wotan, though they are filled with indignation at the irreverence of the Philistines who frankly avow that they find the remarks of the god too often tedious and nonsensical. Now to be devoted to Wagner merely as a dog is devoted to his master, sharing a few elementary ideas, appetites and emotions with him, and, for the rest, reverencing his superiority without understanding it, is no true Wagnerism. Yet nothing better is possible without a stock of ideas common to master and disciple. Unfortunately, the ideas of the revolutionary Wagner of 1848 are taught neither by the education nor the experience of English and American gentleman-amateurs, who are almost always political mugwumps, and hardly ever associate with revolutionists. The earlier attempts to translate his numerous pamphlets and essays into English, resulted in ludicrous mixtures of pure nonsense with the absurdest distortions of his ideas into the ideas of the translators. We now have a translation which is a masterpiece of interpretation and an eminent addition to our literature; but that is not because its author, Mr. Ashton Ellis, knows the German dictionary better than his predecessors.   He is simply in possession of Wagner's ideas. which were to them inconceivable.

All I pretend to do in this book is to impart the ideas which are most likely to be lacking in the conventional Englishman's equipment.   I came by them myself much as Wagner did, having learnt more about music than about anything else in my youth, and sown my political wild oats subsequently in the revolutionary school. This combination is not common in England; and as I seem, so far, to be the only publicly articulate result of it, I venture to add my commentary to what has already been written by musicians who are no revolutionists, and revolutionists who are no musicians.

Pitfold, Hindhead, 1898.   G. B. S.

THE PERFECT
WAGNERITE

PRELIMINARY
ENCOURAGEMENTS

A few of these will be welcome to the ordinary citizen visiting the theatre to satisfy his curiosity, or his desire to be in the fashion, by witnessing a representation of Richard Wagner's famous tetralogy: *The Niblung's Ring*.

First, *The Ring*, with all its gods and giants and dwarfs, its water-maidens and Valkyries, its wishing-cap, magic ring, enchanted sword, and miraculous treasure, is a drama of today, and not of a remote and fabulous antiquity. It could not have been written before the second half of the nineteenth century, because it deals with events which were only then consummating themselves. Unless the spectator recognizes in it an image of the life he is himself fighting his way through, it must needs appear to him a monstrous development of the Christmas pantomimes, spun out here and there into intolerable lengths of dull conversation by the principal baritone. Fortunately, even from this point of view, *The Ring* is full of extraordinarily attractive episodes, both orchestral and dramatic. The nature music alone—music of river and rainbow, fire and forest—is enough to bribe people with any love of the country in them to endure the passages of political philosophy in the sure hope of a prettier page to come. Everybody, too, can enjoy the love music, the hammer and anvil music, the clumping of the giants, the tune of the young woodsman's horn, the trilling of the bird, the dragon music and nightmare music and thunder and lightning music, the profusion of simple melody, the sensuous charm of the orchestration: in short, the vast extent of common ground between *The Ring* and the ordinary music we use for play and pleasure. Hence it is that the four separate music-plays of which it is built have become popular throughout Europe as operas. We shall presently see that one of them, *Night Falls on the Gods*, actually is an opera.

It is generally understood, however, that there is an inner ring of superior persons to whom the whole work has a most urgent and searching philosophic and social significance. I profess to be such a superior person; and I write this pamphlet for the assistance of those who wish to be introduced to the work on equal terms with that inner circle of adepts.

My second encouragement is addressed to modest citizens who may suppose themselves to be disqualified from enjoying *The Ring* by their technical ignorance of music. They may dismiss all such misgivings speedily and confidently. If the sound of music has any power to move them, they will find that Wagner exacts nothing further. There is not a single bar of "classical music" in *The Ring*—not a note in it that has any other point than the single direct point of giving musical expression to the drama. In classical music there are, as the analytical programs tell us, first subjects and second subjects, free fantasias, recapitulations, and codas; there are fugues, with counter-subjects, strettos, and pedal points; there are passacaglias on ground basses, canons ad hypodiapente, and other ingenuities, which have, after all, stood or fallen by their prettiness as much as the simplest folk tune. Wagner is never driving at anything of this sort any more than Shakespeare in his plays is driving at such ingenuities of verse making as sonnets, triolets, and the like. And this is why he is so easy for the natural musician who has had no academic teaching. The professors, when Wagner's music is played to them, exclaim at once "What is this? Is it aria, or recitative? Is there no cabaletta to it—not even a full close? Why was that discord not prepared; and why does he not resolve it correctly? How dare he indulge in those scandalous and illicit transitions into a key that has not one note in common with the key he has just left? Listen to those false relations! What does he want with six drums and eight horns when Mozart worked miracles with two of each? The man is no musician." The layman neither knows nor cares about any of these things. If Wagner were to turn aside from his straightforward dramatic purpose to propitiate the professors with correct exercises in sonata form, his music would at once become unintelligible to the unsophisticated spectator, upon whom the familiar and dreaded "classical" sensation would descend like the influenza. Nothing of the kind need be dreaded. The unskilled, untaught musician may approach Wagner boldly; for there is no possibility of a misunderstanding between them: the *Ring* music is perfectly single and simple. It is the adept musician of the old school who has everything to unlearn; and him I leave, unpitied, to his fate.

THE NIBLUNG'S RING

The Ring consists of four plays, intended to be performed on four successive evenings, entitled *The Rhine Gold* (a prologue to the other three), *The Valkyrie, Siegfried,* and *Night Falls on the Gods;* or, in the original German, *Das Rheingold, Die Walküre, Siegfried,* and *Die Götterdämmerung.*

THE

RHINE GOLD

Let me assume for a moment that you are a young and good-
looking woman. Try to imagine yourself in that character
at Klondyke five years ago. The place is teeming with gold.
If you are content to leave the gold alone, as the wise leave
flowers without plucking them, enjoying with perfect naïveté
its color and glitter and preciousness, no human being will
ever be the worse for your knowledge of it; and whilst you
remain in that frame of mind the golden age will endure.

Now suppose a man comes along: a man who has no
sense of the golden age, nor any power of living in the present:
a man with common desires, cupidities, ambitions, just like
most of the men you know. Suppose you reveal to that man
the fact that if he will only pluck this gold up, and turn it into
money, millions of men, driven by the invisible whip of
hunger, will toil underground and overground night and
day to pile up more and more gold for him until he is master
of the world! You will find that the prospect will not tempt
him so much as you might imagine, because it involves some
distasteful trouble to himself to start with, and because there
is something else within his reach involving no distasteful
toil, which he desires more passionately; and that is yourself. So long as he is preoccupied with love of you, the
gold, and all that it implies, will escape him: the golden

age will endure. Not until he forswears love will he stretch out his hand to the gold, and found the Plutonic empire for himself. But the choice between love and gold may not rest altogether with him. He may be an ugly, ungracious, unamiable person, whose affections may seem merely ludicrous and despicable to you. In that case, you may repulse him, and most bitterly humiliate and disappoint him. What is left to him then but to curse the love he can never win, and turn remorselessly to the gold? With that, he will make short work of your golden age, and leave you lamenting its lost thoughtlessness and sweetness.

In due time the gold of Klondyke will find its way to the great cities of the world. But the old dilemma will keep continually reproducing itself. The man who will turn his back on love, and upon all the fruitful, creative, life-pursuing activities into which the loftiest human energy can develop it, and will set himself single-heartedly to gather gold in an exultant dream of wielding its Plutonic powers, will find the treasure yielding quickly to his touch. But few men will make this sacrifice voluntarily. Not until the Plutonic power is so strongly set up that the higher human impulses are suppressed as rebellious, and even the mere appetites are denied, starved, and insulted when they cannot purchase their satisfaction with gold, are the energetic spirits driven to build their lives upon riches. How inevitable that course has become to us is plain enough to those who have the power of understanding what they see as they look at the plutocratic societies of our modern capitals.

First Scene

Here, then, is the subject of the first scene of *The Rhine Gold*. As you sit waiting for the curtain to rise, you suddenly catch the booming ground-tone of a mighty river. It becomes plainer, clearer: you get nearer to the surface, and catch the green light and the flights of bubbles. Then the curtain goes up and you see what you heard—the depths of the Rhine, with three strange fairy fishes, half water-maidens, singing and enjoying themselves exuberantly. They are not singing barcarolles or ballads about the Lorely and her fated lovers, but simply trolling any nonsense that comes into their heads in time to the dancing of the water and the rhythm of their swimming. It is the golden age; and the attraction of this spot for the Rhine maidens is a lump of the Rhine gold, which they value, in an entirely uncommercial way, for its bodily beauty and splendor. Just at present it is eclipsed, because the sun is not striking down through the water.

Presently there comes a poor devil of a dwarf stealing along the slippery rocks of the river bed, a creature with energy enough to make him strong of body and fierce of passion, but with a brutish narrowness of intelligence and selfishness of imagination: too stupid to see that his own welfare can only be compassed as part of the welfare of the world, too full of brute force not to grab vigorously at his own gain. Such dwarfs are quite common in London. He comes now with a fruitful impulse in him, in search of what he lacks in himself, beauty, lightness of heart, imagination, music. The Rhine maidens, representing all these to him, fill him with hope and longing; and he never considers that he has nothing to offer that they could possibly desire, being by natural limitation incapable of seeing anything from anyone else's point of view. With perfect simplicity, he offers himself as a sweetheart to them. But they are thoughtless, elemental, only half real things, much like modern young ladies. That the poor dwarf is repulsive to their sense of physical beauty and their romantic conception of heroism, that he is ugly and awkward, greedy and ridiculous, disposes for them of his claim to live and love. They mock him atrociously, pretending to fall in love with him at first sight, and then slipping away and making game of him, heaping ridicule and disgust on the poor wretch until he is beside himself with mortification and rage. They forget him when the water begins to glitter in the sun, and the gold to reflect its glory. They break into ecstatic worship of their treasure; and though they know the parable of Klondyke quite well, they have no fear that the gold will be wrenched away by the dwarf, since it will yield to no one who has not forsworn love for it, and it is in pursuit of love that he has come to them. They forget that they have poisoned that desire in him by their mockery and denial of it, and that he now knows that life will give him nothing that he cannot wrest from it by the Plutonic power. It is just as if some poor, rough, vulgar, coarse fellow were to offer to take his part in aristocratic society, and be snubbed into the knowledge that only as a millionaire could he ever hope to bring that society to his feet and buy himself a beautiful and refined wife. His choice is forced on him. He forswears love as thousands of us forswear it every day; and in a moment the gold is in his grasp, and he disappears in the depths, leaving the water-fairies vainly screaming "Stop thief!" whilst the river seems to plunge into darkness and sink from us as we rise to the cloud regions above.

And now, what forces are there in the world to resist Alberic, our dwarf, in his new character of sworn plutocrat? He is soon at work wielding the power of the gold. For his gain, hordes of his fellow-creatures are thenceforth condemned to slave miserably, overground and underground, lashed to their work by the invisible whip of starvation. They never see him, any more than the victims of our "dangerous trades " ever see the shareholders whose power is nevertheless everywhere, driving them to destruction. The very wealth they create with their labor becomes an additional force to impoverish them; for as fast as they make it it slips from their hands into the hands of their master, and makes him mightier

than ever.   You can see the process for yourself in every
civilized country today, where millions of people toil in want
and disease to heap up more wealth for our Alberics, laying
up nothing for themselves, except sometimes horrible and
agonizing disease and the certainty of premature death.
All this part of the story is frightfully real, frightfully present,
frightfully modern; and its effects on our social life are so
ghastly and ruinous that we no longer know enough of
happiness to be discomposed by it.   It is only the poet, with
his vision of what life might be, to whom these things are
unendurable.   If we were a race of poets we would make
an end of them before the end of this miserable century.
Being a race of moral dwarfs instead, we think them highly
respectable, comfortable and proper, and allow them to
breed and multiply their evil in all directions.   If there were
no higher power in the world to work against Alberic, the
end of it would be utter destruction.

Such a force there is, however; and it is called Godhead.
The mysterious thing we call life organizes itself into all
living shapes, bird, beast, beetle and fish, rising to the
human marvel in cunning dwarfs and in laborious muscular
giants, capable, these last, of enduring toil, willing to buy
love and life, not with suicidal curses and renunciations,
but with patient manual drudgery in the service of higher
powers.   And these higher powers are called into existence
by the same self-organization of life still more wonderfully
into rare persons who may by comparison be called gods,
creatures capable of thought, whose aims extend far beyond
the satisfaction of their bodily appetites and personal
affections, since they perceive that it is only by the establishment of a social order founded on common bonds of moral
faith that the world can rise from mere savagery.   But how
is this order to be set up by Godhead in a world of stupid
giants, since these thoughtless ones pursue only their narrower
personal ends and can by no means understand the aims

of a god? Godhead, face to face with Stupidity, must compromise. Unable to enforce on the world the pure law of thought, it must resort to a mechanical law of command-ments to be enforced by brute punishments and the destruc-tion of the disobedient. And however carefully these laws are framed to represent the highest thoughts of the framers at the moment of their promulgation, before a day has elapsed that thought has grown and widened by the ceaseless evolu-tion of life; and lo! yesterday's law already fallen out with today's thought. Yet if the high givers of that law them-selves set the example of breaking it before it is a week old, they destroy all its authority with their subjects, and so break the weapon they have forged to rule them for their own good. They must therefore maintain at all costs the sanctity of the law, even when it has ceased to represent their thought; so that at last they get entangled in a network of ordinances which they no longer believe in, and yet have made so sacred by custom and so terrible by punishment, that they cannot themselves escape from them. Thus Godhead's resort to law finally costs it half its integrity—as if a spiritual king, to gain temporal power, had plucked out one of his eyes—and it finally begins secretly to long for the advent of some power higher than itself which will destroy its artificial empire of law, and establish a true republic of free thought.

This is by no means the only difficulty in the dominion of Law. The brute force for its execution must be pur-chased; and the mass of its subjects must be persuaded to respect the authority which employs this force. But how is such respect to be implanted in them if they are unable to comprehend the thought of the lawgiver? Clearly, only by associating the legislative power with such displays of splendor and majesty as will impress their senses and awe their imaginations. The god turned lawgiver, in short, must be crowned Pontiff and King. Since he cannot be known to the common folk as their superior in wisdom, he must be known to them as their superior in riches, as the dweller in castles, the wearer of gold and purple, the eater of mighty feasts, the commander of armies, and the wielder of powers of life and death, of salvation and damnation after death. Something may be done in this way without corruption whilst the golden age still endures. Your gods may not prevail with the dwarfs; but they may go to these honest giants who will give a day's work for a day's pay, and induce them to build for Godhead a mighty fortress, complete with hall and chapel, tower and bell, for the sake of the homesteads that will grow up in security round that church-castle. This only, however, whilst the golden age lasts. The moment the Plutonic power is let loose, and the loveless Alberic comes into the field with his corrupting millions, the gods are face to face with destruction; since Alberic, able with invisible hunger-whip to force the labor of the dwarfs and to buy the services of the giants, can outshine all the temporal shows and splendors of the golden age, and make himself master of the world, unless the gods, with their bigger brains, can capture his gold. This, the dilemma of the Church today, is the situation created by the exploit of Alberic in the depths of the Rhine.

Second Scene

From the bed of the river we rise into cloudy regions, and finally come out into the clear in a meadow, where Wotan, the god of gods, and his consort Fricka lie sleeping. Wotan, you will observe, has lost one eye; and you will presently learn that he plucked it out voluntarily as the price to be paid for his alliance with Fricka, who in return has brought to him as her dowry all the powers of Law. The meadow is on the brink of a ravine, beyond which, towering on distant heights, stand Godhome, a mighty castle, newly built as a house of state for the one-eyed god and his all-ruling wife. Wotan has not yet seen this castle except in his dreams: two giants have just built it for him whilst he slept; and the reality is before him for the first time when Fricka wakes him. In that majestic burg he is to rule with her and through her over the humble giants, who have eyes to gape at the glorious castles their own hands have built from his design, but no brains to design castles for themselves, or to comprehend divinity. As a god, he is to be great, secure, and mighty; but he is also to be passionless, affectionless, wholly impartial; for Godhead, if it is to live with Law, must have no weaknesses, no respect for persons. All such sweet littlenesses must be left to the humble stupid giants to make their toil sweet to them; and the god must, after all, pay for Olympian power the same price the dwarf has paid for Plutonic power.

Wotan has forgotten this in his dreams of greatness. Not so Fricka. What she is thinking of is this price that Wotan has consented to pay, in token whereof he has promised this day to hand over to the giants Fricka's sister, the goddess Freia, with her golden love-apples. When Fricka reproaches Wotan with having selfishly forgotten this, she finds that he, like herself, is not prepared to go through with his bargain, and that he is trusting to another great world-force, the Lie (a European Power, as Lassalle said), to help him to trick the giants out of their reward. But this force does not dwell in Wotan himself, but in another, a god over whom he has triumphed, one Loki, the god of Intellect, Argument, Imagination, Illusion, and Reason. Loki has promised to deliver him from his contract, and to cheat the giants for him; but he has not arrived to keep his word: indeed, as Fricka bitterly points out, why should not the Lie fail Wotan, since such failure is the very essence of him?

The giants come soon enough; and Freia flies to Wotan for protection against them. Their purposes are quite honest;

and they have no doubt of the god's faith. There stands their part of the contract fulfilled, stone on stone, port and pinnacle all faithfully finished from Wotan's design by their mighty labor. They have come undoubtingly for their agreed wage. Then there happens what is to them an incredible, inconceivable thing. The god begins to shuffle. There are no moments in life more tragic than those in which the humble common man, the manual worker, leaving with implicit trust all high affairs to his betters, and reverencing them wholly as worthy of that trust, even to the extent of accepting as his rightful function the saving of them from all roughening and coarsening drudgeries, first discovers that they are corrupt, greedy, unjust and treacherous. The shock drives a ray of prophetic light into one giant's mind, and gives him a momentary eloquence. In that moment he rises above his stupid gianthood, and earnestly warns the Son of Light that all his power and eminence of priesthood, godhood, and kingship must stand or fall with the unbearable cold greatness of the incorruptible lawgiver. But Wotan, whose assumed character of lawgiver is altogether false to his real passionate nature, despises the rebuke; and the giant's ray of insight is lost in the murk of his virtuous indignation.

In the midst of the wrangle, Loki comes at last, excusing himself for being late on the ground that he has been detained by a matter of importance which he has promised to lay before Wotan. When pressed to give his mind to the business immediately in hand, and to extricate Wotan from his dilemma, he has nothing to say except that the giants are evidently altogether in the right. The castle has been duly built: he has tried every stone of it, and found the work first-rate: there is nothing to be done but pay the price agreed upon by handing over Freia to the giants. The gods are furious; and Wotan passionately declares that he only consented to the bargain on Loki's promise to find a way for him out of it. But Loki says no: he has promised to find a

way out if any such way exist, but not to make a way if there
is no way. He has wandered over the whole earth in
search of some treasure great enough to buy Freia back from
the giants; but in all the world he has found nothing for
which Man will give up Woman. And this, by the way,
reminds him of the matter he had promised to lay before
Wotan. The Rhine maidens have complained to him of
Alberic's theft of their gold; and he mentions it as a curious
exception to his universal law of the unpurchasable preciousness of love, that this gold-robber has forsworn love for the
sake of the fabulous riches of the Plutonic empire and the
mastery of the world through its power.

No sooner is the tale told than the giants stoop lower than
the dwarf. Alberic forswore love only when it was denied
to him and made the instrument for cruelly murdering his
self-respect. But the giants, with love within their reach,
with Freia and her golden apples in their hands, offer to
give her up for the treasure of Alberic. Observe, it is the
treasure alone that they desire. They have no fierce dreams
of dominion over their superiors, or of moulding the world
to any conceptions of their own. They are neither clever
nor ambitious: they simply covet money. Alberic's gold:
that is their demand, or else Freia, as agreed upon, whom
they now carry off as hostage, leaving Wotan to consider
their ultimatum.

Freia gone, the gods begin to wither and age: her golden
apples, which they so lightly bargained away, they now find
to be a matter of life and death to them; for not even the gods
can live on Law and Godhead alone, be their castles ever so
splendid. Loki alone is unaffected: the Lie, with all its
cunning wonders, its glistenings and shiftings and mirages, is
a mere appearance: it has no body and needs no food.
What is Wotan to do? Loki sees the answer clearly
enough: he must bluntly rob Alberic. There is nothing
to prevent him except moral scruple; for Alberic, after all,

is a poor, dim, dwarfed, credulous creature whom a god can outsee and a lie can outwit. Down, then, Wotan and Loki plunge into the mine where Alberic's slaves are piling up wealth for him under the invisible whip.

Third Scene

This gloomy place need not be a mine: it might just as well be a match-factory, with yellow phosphorus, phossy jaw, a large dividend, and plenty of clergymen shareholders. Or it might be a whitelead factory, or a chemical works, or a pottery, or a railway shunting yard, or a tailoring shop, or a little gin-sodden laundry, or a bakehouse, or a big shop, or any other of the places where human life and welfare are daily sacrificed in order that some greedy foolish creature may be able to hymn exultantly to his Plutonic idol:

> Thou mak'st me eat whilst others starve,
> And sing while others do lament:
> Such unto me Thy blessings are,
> As if I were Thine only care.

In the mine, which resounds with the clinking anvils of the dwarfs toiling miserably to heap up treasure for their master, Alberic has set his brother Mime—more familiarly, Mimmy—to make him a helmet. Mimmy dimly sees that there is some magic in this helmet, and tries to keep it; but Alberic wrests it from him, and shows him, to his cost, that it is the veil of the invisible whip, and that he who wears it can appear in what shape he will, or disappear from view altogether. This helmet is a very common article in our streets, where it generally takes the form of a tall hat. It makes a man invisible as a shareholder, and changes him into various shapes, such as a pious Christian, a subscriber to hospitals, a benefactor of the poor, a model husband and

father, a shrewd, practical, independent Englishman, and
what not, when he is really a pitiful parasite on the commonwealth, consuming a great deal, and producing nothing,
feeling nothing, knowing nothing, believing nothing, and
doing nothing except what all the rest do, and that only
because he is afraid not to do it, or at least pretend to
do it.

When Wotan and Loki arrive, Loki claims Alberic as an
old acquaintance. But the dwarf has no faith in these civil
strangers: Greed instinctively mistrusts Intellect, even in
the garb of Poetry and the company of Godhead, whilst
envying the brilliancy of the one and the dignity of the other.
Alberic breaks out at them with a terrible boast of the power
now within his grasp. He paints for them the world as it
will be when his dominion over it is complete, when the soft
airs and green mosses of its valleys shall be changed into
smoke, slag, and filth; when slavery, disease, and squalor,
soothed by drunkenness and mastered by the policeman's
baton, shall become the foundation of society; and when
nothing shall escape ruin except such pretty places and
pretty women as he may like to buy for the slaking of his own
lusts. In that kingdom of evil he sees that there will be no
power but his own. These gods, with their moralities and
legalities and intellectual subtlety, will go under and be
starved out of existence. He bids Wotan and Loki beware
of it; and his "Hab' Acht!" is hoarse, horrible, and sinister.
Wotan is revolted to the very depths of his being: he cannot
stifle the execration that bursts from him. But Loki is
unaffected: he has no moral passion: indignation is as
absurd to him as enthusiasm. He finds it exquisitely
amusing—having a touch of the comic spirit in him—that
the dwarf, in stirring up the moral fervor of Wotan, has
removed his last moral scruple about becoming a thief.
Wotan will now rob the dwarf without remorse; for is it not
positively his highest duty to take this power out of such evil

hands and use it himself in the interests of Godhead? On the loftiest moral grounds, he lets Loki do his worst.

A little cunningly disguised flattery makes short work of Alberic. Loki pretends to be afraid of him; and he swallows that bait unhesitatingly. But how, enquires Loki, is he to guard against the hatred of his million slaves? Will they not steal from him, whilst he sleeps, the magic ring, the symbol of his power, which he has forged from the gold of the Rhine? "You think yourself very clever," sneers Alberic, and then begins to boast of the enchantments of the magic helmet. Loki refuses to believe in such marvels without witnessing them. Alberic, only too glad to shew off his powers, puts on the helmet and transforms himself into a monstrous serpent. Loki gratifies him by pretending to be frightened out of his wits, but ventures to remark that it would be better still if the helmet could transform its owner into some tiny creature that could hide and spy in the smallest cranny. Alberic promptly transforms himself into a toad. In an instant Wotan's foot is on him; Loki tears away the helmet; they pinion him, and drag him away a prisoner up through the earth to the meadow by the castle.

Fourth Scene

There, to pay for his freedom, he has to summon his slaves from the depths to place all the treasure they have heaped up for him at the feet of Wotan. Then he demands his liberty; but Wotan must have the ring as well. And here the dwarf, like the giant before him, feels the very foundations of the world shake beneath him at the discovery of his own base cupidity in a higher power. That evil should, in its loveless desperation, create malign powers which Godhead could not create, seems but natural justice to him. But that Godhead should steal those malign powers from evil, and wield them itself, is a monstrous perversion;

and his appeal to Wotan to forego it is almost terrible in its conviction of wrong. It is of no avail. Wotan falls back again on virtuous indignation. He reminds Alberic that he stole the gold from the Rhine daughters, and takes the attitude of the just judge compelling a restitution of stolen goods. Alberic, knowing perfectly well that the judge is taking the goods to put them in his own pocket, has the ring torn from his finger, and is once more as poor as he was when he came slipping and stumbling among the slimy rocks in the bed of the Rhine.

This is the way of the world. In older times, when the Christian laborer was drained dry by the knightly spend-thrift, and the spendthrift was drained by the Jewish usurer, Church and State, religion and law, seized on the Jew and drained him as a Christian duty. When the forces of lovelessness and greed had built up our own sordid capitalist systems, driven by invisible proprietorship, robbing the poor, defacing the earth, and forcing themselves as a universal curse even on the generous and humane, then religion and law and intellect, which would never themselves have dis-covered such systems, their natural bent being towards welfare, economy, and life instead of towards corruption, waste, and death, nevertheless did not scruple to seize by fraud and force these powers of evil on pretence of using them for good. And it inevitably happens that when the Church, the Law, and all the Talents have made common cause to rob the people, the Church is far more vitally harmed by that unfaithfulness to itself than its more mechan-ical confederates; so that finally they turn on their discredited ally and rob the Church, with the cheerful co-operation of Loki, as in France and Italy for instance.

The twin giants come back with their hostage, in whose presence Godhead blooms again. The gold is ready for them; but now that the moment has come for parting with Freia the gold does not seem so tempting; and they are

sorely loth to let her go. Not unless there is gold enough to
utterly hide her from them—not until the heap has grown so
that they can see nothing but gold—until money has come
between them and every human feeling, will they part with
her. There is not gold enough to accomplish this: however
cunningly Loki spreads it, the glint of Freia's hair is still
visible to Giant Fafnir, and the magic helmet must go on the
heap to shut it out. Even then Fafnir's brother, Fasolt,
can catch a beam from her eye through a chink, and is
rendered incapable thereby of forswearing her. There is
nothing to stop that chink but the ring; and Wotan is as
greedily bent on keeping that as Alberic himself was; nor
can the other gods persuade him that Freia is worth it,
since for the highest god, love is not the highest good, but
only the universal delight that bribes all living things to
travail with renewed life. Life itself, with its accomplished
marvels and its infinite potentialities, is the only force that
Godhead can worship. Wotan does not yield until he is
reached by the voice of the fruitful earth, that before he or
the dwarfs or the giants or the Law or the Lie or any of these
things were, had the seed of them all in her bosom, and the
seed perhaps of something higher even than himself, that
shall one day supersede him and cut the tangles and alliances
and compromises that already have cost him one of his eyes.
When Erda, the First Mother of life, rises from her sleeping-
place in the heart of the earth, and warns him to yield the
ring, he obeys her; the ring is added to the heap of gold;
and all sense of Freia is cut off from the giants.

But now what Law is left to these two poor stupid laborers
whereby one shall yield to the other any of the treasure for
which they have each paid the whole price in surrendering
Freia? They look by mere habit to the god to judge for
them; but he, with his heart stirring towards higher forces
than himself, turns with disgust from these lower forces.
They settle it as two wolves might; and Fafnir batters his

brother dead with his staff.   It is a horrible thing to see and
hear, to anyone who knows how much blood has been shed
in the world in just that way by its brutalized toilers, honest
fellows enough until their betters betrayed them.   Fafnir
goes off with his booty.   It is quite useless to him.   He has
neither the cunning nor the ambition to establish the Plutonic
empire with it.   Merely to prevent others from getting it is
the only purpose it brings him.   He piles it in a cave;
transforms himself into a dragon by the helmet; and devotes
his life to guarding it, as much a slave to it as a jailor is to his
prisoner.   He had much better have thrown it all back
into the Rhine and transformed himself into the shortest-
lived animal that enjoys at least a brief run in the sunshine.
His case, however, is far too common to be surprising.   The
world is overstocked with persons who sacrifice all their
affections, and madly trample and batter down their fellows
to obtain riches of which, when they get them, they are
unable to make the smallest use, and to which they become
the most miserable slaves.

  The gods soon forget Fafnir in their rejoicing over Freia.
Donner, the Thunder god, springs to a rocky summit and
calls the clouds as a shepherd calls his flocks.   They come
at his summons; and he and the castle are hidden by their
black legions.   Froh, the Rainbow god, hastens to his side.
At the stroke of Donner's hammer the black murk is riven in
all directions by darting ribbons of lightning; and as the
air clears, the castle is seen in its fullest splendor, accessible
now by the rainbow bridge which Froh has cast across the
ravine.   In the glory of this moment Wotan has a great
thought.   With all his aspirations to establish a reign of
noble thought, of righteousness, order, and justice, he has
found that day that there is no race yet in the world that
quite spontaneously, naturally, and unconsciously realizes
his ideal.   He himself has found how far short Godhead falls
of the thing it conceives.   He, the greatest of gods, has

been unable to control his fate: he has been forced against his will to choose between evils, to make disgraceful bargains, to break them still more disgracefully, and even then to see the price of his disgrace slip through his fingers. His consort has cost him half his vision; his castle has cost him his affections; and the attempt to retain both has cost him his honor. On every side he is shackled and bound, dependent on the laws of Fricka and on the lies of Loki, forced to traffic with dwarfs for handicraft and with giants for strength, and to pay them both in false coin. After all, a god is a pitiful thing. But the fertility of the First Mother is not yet exhausted. The life that came from her has ever climbed up to a higher and higher organization. From toad and serpent to dwarf, from bear and elephant to giant, from dwarf and giant to a god with thoughts, with comprehension of the world, with ideals. Why should it stop there? Why should it not rise from the god to the Hero? to the creature in whom the god's unavailing thought shall have become effective will and life, who shall make his way straight to truth and reality over the laws of Fricka and the lies of Loki with a strength that overcomes giants and a cunning that outwits dwarfs? Yes: Erda, the First Mother, must travail again, and breed him a race of heroes to deliver the world and himself from his limited powers and disgraceful bargains. This is the vision that flashes on him as he turns to the rainbow bridge and calls his wife to come and dwell with him in Valhalla, the home of the gods.

They are all overcome with Valhalla's glory except Loki. He is behind the scenes of this joint reign of the Divine and the Legal. He despises these gods with their ideals and their golden apples. "I am ashamed," he says, "to have dealings with these futile creatures." And so he follows them to the rainbow bridge. But as they set foot on it, from the river below rises the wailing of the Rhine daughters for their lost gold.   "You down there in the water," cries Loki with brutal irony: "you used to bask in the glitter of your gold: henceforth you shall bask in the splendor of the gods." And they reply that the truth is in the depths and the darkness, and that what blazes on high there is falsehood.   And with that the gods pass into their glorious stronghold.

WAGNER AS
REVOLUTIONIST

Before leaving this explanation of *The Rhine Gold*, I must have a word or two about it with the reader.

It is the least popular of the sections of *The Ring*. The reason is that its dramatic moments lie quite outside the consciousness of people whose joys and sorrows are all domestic and personal, and whose religions and political ideas are purely conventional and superstitious. To them it is a struggle between half a dozen fairytale personages for a ring, involving hours of scolding and cheating, and one long scene in a dark, gruesome mine, with gloomy, ugly music, and not a glimpse of a handsome young man or pretty woman. Only those of wider consciousness can follow it breathlessly, seeing in it the whole tragedy of human history and the whole horror of the dilemmas from which the world is shrinking today. At Bayreuth I have seen a party of English tourists, after enduring agonies of boredom from Alberic, rise in the middle of the third scene, and almost force their way out of the dark theatre into the sunlit pine-wood without. And I have seen people who were deeply affected by the scene driven almost beside themselves by this disturbance. But it was a very natural thing for the unfortunate tourists to do, since in this *Rhine Gold* prologue there is no interval between the acts for escape. Roughly speaking, people who have no general ideas, no touch of the concern of the philosopher and statesman for the race, cannot enjoy *The Rhine Gold* as a drama. They may find compensations in some exceedingly pretty music, at times even grand and glorious, which will enable them to escape occasionally from the struggle between Alberic and Wotan; but if their capacity for music should be as limited as their comprehension of the world, they had better stay away.

And now, attentive Reader, we have reached the point at which some foolish person is sure to interrupt us by declaring that *The Rhine Gold* is what they call "a work of art" pure and simple, and that Wagner never dreamt of shareholders, tall hats, whitelead factories, and industrial and political questions looked at from the socialist and humanitarian points of view. We need not discuss these impertinences: it is easier to silence them with the facts of Wagner's life. In 1843 he obtained the position of conductor of the Opera at Dresden at a salary of £225 a year, with a pension. This was a first-rate permanent appointment in the service of the Saxon State, carrying an assured professional position and livelihood with it. In 1848, the year of revolutions, the discontented middle class, unable to rouse the Church-and-State governments of the day from their bondage to custom, caste, and law by appeals to morality or constitutional agitation for Liberal reforms, made common cause with the starving wage-working class, and resorted to armed rebellion, which reached Dresden in 1849. Had Wagner been the mere musical epicure and political mugwump that the term "artist" seems to suggest to so many critics and amateurs—that is, a creature in their own lazy likeness—he need have taken no more part in the political struggles of his day than Bishop took in the English Reform agitation of 1832, or Sterndale Bennett in the Chartist or Free Trade movements. What he did do was first to make a desperate appeal to the King to cast off his bonds and answer the need of the time by taking true kingship on himself and leading his people to the redress of their intolerable wrongs (fancy the poor monarch's feelings!), and then, when the crash came, to take his side with the right and the poor against the rich and the wrong. When the insurrection was defeated, three leaders of it were especially marked down for vengeance: August Roeckel, an old friend of Wagner's to whom he wrote a well-known series of letters; Michael Bakoonin, afterwards a famous apostle of revolutionary Anarchism; and Wagner himself. Wagner escaped to Switzerland: Roeckel and Bakoonin suffered long terms of imprisonment. Wagner was of course utterly ruined, pecuniarily and socially (to his own intense relief and satisfaction); and his exile lasted twelve years. His first idea was to get his *Tannhäuser* produced in Paris. With the notion of explaining himself to the Parisians he wrote a pamphlet entitled *Art and Revolution*, a glance through which will show how thoroughly the socialistic side of the revolution had his sympathy, and how completely he had got free from the influence of the established Churches of his day. For three years he kept pouring forth pamphlets—some of them elaborate treatises in size and intellectual rank, but still essentially the pamphlets and manifestoes of a born agitator —on social evolution, religion, life, art and the influence of riches. In 1853, the poem of *The Ring* was privately printed; and in 1854, five years after the Dresden insurrection, the *Rhine Gold* score was completed to the last drum tap.

These facts are on official record in Germany, where the proclamation summing up Wagner as "a politically dangerous person" may be consulted to this day. The pamphlets are now accessible to English readers in the translation of Mr. Ashton Ellis. This being so, any person who, having perhaps heard that I am a Socialist, attempts to persuade you that my interpretation of *The Rhine Gold* is only "my socialism" read into the works of a dilettantist who borrowed an idle tale from an old saga to make an opera book with, may safely be dismissed from your consideration as an ignoramus.

If you are now satisfied that *The Rhine Gold* is an allegory, do not forget that an allegory is never quite consistent except when it is written by someone without dramatic faculty, in which case it is unreadable. There is only one way of dramatizing an idea; and that is by putting on the stage a human being possessed by that idea, yet none the less a human being with all the human impulses which make him akin and therefore interesting to us. Bunyan, in his *Pilgrim's Progress*, does not, like his unread imitators, attempt to personify Christianity and Valour: he dramatizes for you the life of the Christian and the Valiant Man. Just so, though I have shown that Wotan is Godhead and Kingship, and Loki, Logic and Imagination without living Will (Brain without Heart, to put it vulgarly); yet in the drama Wotan is a religiously moral man, and Loki a witty, ingenious, imaginative and cynical one. As to Fricka, who stands for State Law, she does not assume her allegorical character in *The Rhine Gold* at all, but is simply Wotan's wife and Freia's sister: nay, she contradicts her allegorical self by conniving at all Wotan's rogueries. That, of course, is just what State Law would do; but we must not save the credit of the allegory by a quip. Not until she reappears in the next play (*The Valkyrie*) does her function in the allegorical scheme become plain.

One preconception will bewilder the spectator hopelessly unless he has been warned against it or is naturally free from it. In the old-fashioned orders of creation, the supernatural personages are invariably conceived as greater than man, for good or evil. In the modern humanitarian order as adopted by Wagner, Man is the highest. In *The Rhine Gold*, it is pretended that there are as yet no men on the earth. There are dwarfs, giants, and gods. The danger is that you will jump to the conclusion that the gods, at least, are a higher order than the human order. On the contrary, the world is waiting for Man to redeem it from the lame and cramped government of the gods. Once grasp that; and the allegory becomes simple enough. Really, of course, the dwarfs, giants, and gods are dramatizations of the three main orders of men: to wit, the instinctive, predatory, lustful, greedy people; the patient, toiling, stupid, respectful, money-worshipping people; and the intellectual, moral, talented people who devise and administer States and Churches. History shows us only one order higher than the highest of these: namely, the order of Heroes.

Now it is quite clear—though you have perhaps never thought of it—that if the next generation of Englishmen consisted wholly of Julius Cæsars, all our political, ecclesiastical, and moral institutions would vanish, and the less perishable of their appurtenances be classed with Stonehenge and the cromlechs and round towers as inexplicable relics of a bygone social order. Julius Cæsars would no more trouble themselves about such contrivances as our codes and churches than a Fellow of the Royal Society will touch his hat to the squire and listen to the village curate's sermons. This is precisely what must happen some day if life continues thrusting towards higher and higher organization as it has hitherto done. As most of our English professional men are to Australian bushmen, so, we must suppose, will the average man of some future day be to Julius Cæsar. Let any man of middle age, pondering this prospect, consider what has happened within a single generation to the articles of faith his father regarded as eternal, nay, to the very scepticisms and blasphemies of his youth (Bishop Colenso's criticism of the Pentateuch, for example!); and he will begin to realize how much of our barbarous Theology and Law the man of

the future will do without. Bakoonin, the Dresden revolutionary leader with whom Wagner went out in 1849, put
forward later on a program, often quoted with foolish
horror, for the abolition of all institutions, religious, political,
juridical, financial, legal, academic, and so on, so as to
leave the will of man free to find its own way. All the
loftiest spirits of that time were burning to raise Man up,
to give him self-respect, to shake him out of his habit of
grovelling before the ideals created by his own imagination,
of attributing the good that sprang from the ceaseless energy
of the life within himself to some superior power in the
clouds, and of making a fetish of self-sacrifice to justify his
own cowardice.

Farther on in *The Ring* we shall see the Hero arrive and
make an end of dwarfs, giants, and gods. Meanwhile, let
us not forget that godhood means to Wagner infirmity and
compromise, and manhood strength and integrity. Above
all, we must understand—for it is the key to much that we
are to see—that the god, since his desire is toward a higher
and fuller life, must long in his inmost soul for the advent
of that greater power whose first work, though this he does
not see as yet, must be his own undoing.

In the midst of all these far-reaching ideas, it is amusing
to find Wagner still full of his ingrained theatrical professionalism, and introducing effects which now seem old-
fashioned and stagey with as much energy and earnestness
as if they were his loftiest inspirations. When Wotan wrests
the ring from Alberic, the dwarf delivers a lurid and blood-
curdling stage curse, calling down on its every future
possessor care, fear, and death. The musical phrase
accompanying this outburst was a veritable harmonic and
melodic bogey to mid-century ears, though time has now
robbed it of its terrors. It sounds again when Fafnir slays
Fasolt, and on every subsequent occasion when the ring
brings death to its holder. This episode must justify itself

purely as a piece of stage sensationalism. On deeper ground it is superfluous and confusing, as the ruin to which the pursuit of riches leads needs no curse to explain it; nor is there any sense in investing Alberic with providential powers in the matter.

THE
VALKYRIE

Before the curtain rises on *The Valkyrie*, let us see what has happened since it fell on *The Rhine Gold*. The persons of the drama will tell us presently; but as we probably do not understand German, that may not help us.

Wotan is still ruling the world in glory from his giant-built castle with his wife Fricka. But he has no security for the continuance of his reign, since Alberic may at any moment contrive to recover the ring, the full power of which he can wield because he has forsworn love. Such forswearing is not possible to Wotan: love, though not his highest need, is a higher need than gold: otherwise he would be no god. Beside, as we have seen, his power has been established in the world by and as a system of laws enforced by penalties. These he must consent to be bound by himself; for a god who broke his own laws would betray the fact that legality and conformity are not the highest rule of conduct—a discovery fatal to his supremacy as Pontiff and Lawgiver. Hence he may not wrest the ring unlawfully from Fafnir, even if he could bring himself to forswear love.

In this insecurity he has hit on the idea of forming a heroic bodyguard. He has trained his love children as war-maidens (Valkyries) whose duty it is to sweep through battlefields and bear away to Valhalla the souls of the bravest who fall there. Thus reinforced by a host of warriors, he has thoroughly indoctrinated them, Loki helping him as dialectician-in-chief, with the conventional system of law and duty, supernatural religion and self-sacrificing idealism, which they believe to be the essence of his godhood, but which is really only the machinery of the love of necessary power which is his mortal weakness. This process secures their fanatical devotion to his system of government; but he knows perfectly well that such systems, in spite of their moral pretensions, serve selfish and ambitious tyrants better than benevolent despots, and that, if once Albéric gets the ring back, he will easily out-Valhalla Valhalla, if not buy it over as a going concern. The only chance of permanent security, then, is the appearance in the world of a hero who, without any illicit prompting from Wotan, will destroy Alberic and wrest the ring from Fafnir. There will then, he believes, be no further cause for anxiety, since he does not yet conceive Heroism as a force hostile to Godhead. In his longing for a rescuer, it does not occur to him that when the Hero comes, his first exploit must be to sweep the gods and their ordinances from the path of the heroic will.

Indeed, he feels that in his own Godhead is the germ of such Heroism, and that from himself the Hero must spring. He takes to wandering, mostly in search of love, from Fricka and Valhalla. He seeks the First Mother; and through her womb, eternally fertile, the inner true thought that made him first a god is reborn as his daughter, uncorrupted by his ambition, unfettered by his machinery of power and his alliances with Fricka and Loki. This daughter, the Valkyrie Brynhild, is his true will, his real self (as he thinks): to her he may say what he must not say to anyone, since in speaking to her he but speaks to himself. "Was Keinem in Worten ich künde," he says to her, "unausgesprochen bleib' es denn ewig: mit mir nur rath' ich, red' ich zu dir."

But from Brynhild no hero can spring until there is a man of Wotan's race to breed with her. Wotan wanders further; and a mortal woman bears him twins: a son and a daughter. He separates them by letting the girl fall into the hands of a forest tribe which in due time gives her as wife to a fierce chief, one Hunding. With the son he himself leads the life of a wolf, and teaches him the only power a god can teach, the power of doing without happiness. When he has given him this terrible training, he abandons him, and goes to the bridal feast of his daughter Sieglinda and Hunding. In the blue cloak of the wanderer, wearing the broad hat that flaps over the socket of his forfeited eye, he appears in Hunding's house, the middle pillar of which is a mighty tree. Into that tree, without a word, he strikes a sword up to the hilt, so that only the might of a hero can withdraw it. Then he goes out as silently as he came, blind to the truth that no weapon from the armory of Godhead can serve the turn of the true Human Hero. Neither Hunding nor any of his guests can move the sword; and there it stays awaiting the destined hand. That is the history of the generations between *The Rhine Gold* and *The Valkyrie*.

The First Act

This time, as we sit looking expectantly at the curtain, we hear, not the deep booming of the Rhine, but the patter of a forest downpour, accompanied by the mutter of a storm which soon gathers into a roar and culminates in crashing thunderbolts. As it passes off, the curtain rises; and there is no mistaking whose forest habitation we are in; for the central pillar is a mighty tree, and the place fit for the dwelling of a fierce chief. The door opens; and an exhausted man reels in: an adept from the school of unhappiness. Sieglinda finds him lying on the hearth. He explains that he has been in a fight; that his weapons, not being as strong as his arms, were broken; and that he had to fly. He desires some drink and a moment's rest; then he will go; for he is an unlucky person, and does not want to bring his ill-luck on the woman who is succoring him. But she, it appears, is also unhappy; and a strong sympathy springs up between them. When her husband arrives, he observes not only this sympathy, but a resemblance between them, a gleam of the snake in their eyes. They sit down to table; and the stranger tells them his unlucky story. He is the son of Wotan, who is known to him only as Wolfing, of the race of the Volsungs. The earliest thing he remembers is returning from a hunt with his father to find their home destroyed, his mother murdered, and his twin-sister carried off. This was the work of a tribe called the Neidings, upon whom he and Wolfing thenceforth waged implacable war until the day when his father disappeared, leaving no trace of himself but an empty wolfskin. The young Volsung was thus cast alone upon the world, finding most hands against him, and bringing no good luck even to his friends. His latest exploit has been the slaying of certain brothers who were forcing their sister to wed against her will. The result has been the slaughter of the woman by her brothers' clansmen, and his own narrow escape by flight.

His luck on this occasion is even worse than he supposes; for Hunding, by whose hearth he has taken refuge, is clansman to the slain brothers and is bound to avenge them. He tells the Volsung that in the morning, weapons or no weapons, he must fight for his life. Then he orders the woman to bed, and follows her himself, taking his spear with him.

The unlucky stranger, left brooding by the hearth, has nothing to console himself with but an old promise of his father's that he shall find a weapon to his hand when he most needs one. The last flicker of the dying fire strikes on the golden hilt of the sword that sticks in the tree; but he does not see it; and the embers sink into blackness. Then the woman returns. Hunding is safely asleep; she has drugged him. She tells the story of the one-eyed man who appeared at her forced marriage, and of the sword. She has always felt, she says, that her miseries will end in the arms of the hero who shall succeed in drawing it forth. The stranger, diffident as he is about his luck, has no misgivings as to his strength and destiny. He gives her his affection at once, and abandons himself to the charm of the night and the season; for it is the beginning of spring. They soon learn from their confidences that she is his stolen twin-sister. He is transported to find that the heroic race of the Volsungs need neither perish nor be corrupted by a lower strain. Hailing the sword by the name of Nothung (or Needed), he plucks it from the tree as her bride-gift, and then, crying, "Both bride and sister be of thy brother; and blossom the blood of the Volsungs!" clasps her as the mate the spring has brought him.

The Second Act

So far, Wotan's plan seems prospering. In the mountains he calls his war-maiden Brynhild, the child borne to him by the First Mother, and bids her see to it that Hunding shall fall in the approaching combat. But he is reckoning without his consort, Fricka. What will she, the Law, say to the lawless pair who have heaped incest on adultery? A hero may have defied the law, and put his own will in its place; but can a god hold him guiltless, when the whole power of the gods can enforce itself only by law? Fricka, shuddering with horror, outraged in every instinct, comes clamoring for punishment. Wotan pleads the general necessity of encouraging heroism in order to keep up the Valhalla bodyguard; but his remonstrances only bring upon

him torrents of reproaches for his own unfaithfulness to the
law in roaming through the world and begetting war-
maidens, "wolfcubs," and the like.   He is hopelessly beaten
in the argument.   Fricka is absolutely right when she declares that the ending of the gods began when he brought
this wolf-hero into the world; and now, to save their very
existence, she pitilessly demands his destruction.   Wotan
has no power to refuse: it is Fricka's mechanical force, and
not his thought, that really rules the world.   He has to recall
Brynhild; take back his former instructions; and ordain that
Hunding shall slay the Volsung.

But now comes another difficulty.   Brynhild is the inner
thought and will of Godhead, the aspiration from the high
life to the higher that is its divine element, and only becomes
separated from it when its resort to kingship and priestcraft
for the sake of temporal power has made it false to itself.
Hitherto, Brynhild, as Valkyrie or hero chooser, has obeyed
Wotan implicitly, taking her work as the holiest and bravest
in his kingdom; and now he tells her what he could not tell
Fricka—what indeed he could not tell to Brynhild, were she
not, as she says, his own will—the whole story of Alberic and
of that inspiration about the raising up of a hero.   She
thoroughly approves of the inspiration; but when the story
ends in the assumption that she too must obey Fricka, and
help Fricka's vassal, Hunding, to undo the great work and
strike the hero down, she for the first time hesitates to accept
his command.   In his fury and despair he overawes her by
the most terrible threats of his anger; and she submits.

Then comes the Volsung Siegmund, following his sister
bride, who has fled into the mountains in a revulsion of
horror at having allowed herself to bring her hero to shame.
Whilst she is lying exhausted and senseless in his arms,
Brynhild appears to him and solemnly warns him that he
must presently leave the earth with her.   He asks whither
he must follow her.   To Valhalla, to take his place there

among the heroes. He asks, shall he find his father there? Yes. Shall he find a wife there? Yes: he will be waited on by beautiful wish-maidens. Shall he meet his sister there? No. Then, says Siegmund, I will not come with you. She tries to make him understand that he cannot help himself. Being a hero, he will not be so persuaded: he has his father's sword, and does not fear Hunding. But when she tells him that she comes from his father, and that the sword of a god will not avail in the hands of a hero, he accepts his fate, but will shape it with his own hand, both for himself and his sister, by slaying her, and then killing himself with the last stroke of the sword. And thereafter he will go to Hell, rather than to Valhalla.

How now can Brynhild, being what she is, choose her side freely in a conflict between this hero and the vassal of Fricka? By instinct she at once throws Wotan's command to the winds, and bids Siegmund nerve himself for the combat with Hunding, in which she pledges him the protection of her shield. The horn of Hunding is soon heard; and Siegmund's spirits rise to fighting pitch at once. The two meet; and the Valkyrie's shield is held before the hero. But when he delivers his sword-stroke at his foe, the weapon shivers on the spear of Wotan, who suddenly appears between them; and the first of the race of heroes falls with the weapon of the Law's vassal through his breast. Brynhild snatches the fragments of the broken sword, and flies, carrying off the woman with her on her war-horse; and Wotan, in terrible wrath, slays Hunding with a wave of his hand, and starts in pursuit of his disobedient daughter.

The Third Act

On a rocky peak, four of the Valkyries are waiting for the rest. The absent ones soon arrive, galloping through the air with slain heroes, gathered from the battlefield, hanging over their saddles.   Only, Brynhild, who comes last, has for her spoil a live woman.   When her eight sisters learn that she has defied Wotan, they dare not help her; and Brynhild has to rouse Sieglinda to make an effort to save herself, by reminding her that she bears in her the seed of a hero, and must face everything, endure anything, sooner than let that seed miscarry.   Sieglinda, in a transport of exaltation, takes the fragments of the sword and flies into the forest.   Then Wotan comes; the sisters fly in terror at his command; and he is left alone with Brynhild.

Here, then, we have the first of the inevitable moments which Wotan did not foresee.   Godhead has now established its dominion over the world by a mighty Church, compelling obedience through its ally the Law, with its formidable State organization of force of arms and cunning of brain.   It has submitted to this alliance to keep the Plutonic power in check—built it up primarily for the sake of that soul in itself which cares only to make the highest better and the best higher; and now here is that very soul separated from it and working for the destruction of its indispensable ally, the lawgiving State.   How is the rebel to be disarmed? Slain it cannot be by Godhead, since it is still Godhead's own very dearest soul.   But hidden, stifled, silenced it must be; or it will wreck the State and leave the Church defenceless.   Not until it passes completely away from Godhead, and is reborn as the soul of the hero, can it work anything but the confusion and destruction of the existing order. How is the world to be protected against it in the meantime? Clearly Loki's help is needed here: it is the Lie that must, on the highest principles, hide the Truth.   Let Loki surround this mountain top with the appearance of a consuming fire; and who will dare penetrate to Brynhild?   It is true that if any man will walk boldly into that fire, he will discover it at once to be a lie, an illusion, a mirage through which he might carry a sack of gunpowder without being a penny the worse. Therefore let the fire seem so terrible that only the hero, when in the fulness of time he appears upon earth, will venture through it; and the problem is solved. Wotan, with a breaking heart, takes leave of Brynhild; throws her into a deep sleep; covers her with her long war-shield; summons Loki, who comes in the shape of a wall of fire surrounding the mountain peak; and turns his back on Brynhild for ever.

The allegory here is happily not so glaringly obvious to the younger generations of our educated classes as it was forty years ago. In those days, any child who expressed a doubt as to the absolute truth of the Church's teaching, even to the extent of asking why Joshua told the sun to stand still instead of telling the earth to cease turning, or of pointing out that a whale's throat would hardly have been large enough to swallow Jonah, was unhesitatingly told that if it harboured such doubts it would spend all eternity after its death in horrible torments in a lake of burning brimstone. It is difficult to write or read this nowadays without laughing; yet no doubt millions of ignorant and credulous people are still teaching their children that. When Wagner himself was a little child, the fact that hell was a fiction devised for the intimidation and subjection of the masses, was a well-kept secret of the thinking and governing classes. At that time the fires of Loki were a very real terror to all, except persons of exceptional force of character and intrepidity of thought. Even thirty years after Wagner had printed the verses of *The Ring* for private circulation, we find him excusing himself from perfectly explicit denial of current superstitions, by reminding his readers that it would expose him to prosecution. In England, so many of our respectable voters are still grovelling in a gloomy devil worship, of which the fires of Loki are the main bulwark, that no Government has yet had the conscience or the courage to repeal our monstrous laws against "blasphemy."

SIEGFRIED

Sieglinda, when she flies into the forest with the hero's son unborn in her womb, and the broken pieces of his sword in her hand, finds shelter in the smithy of a dwarf, where she brings forth her child and dies.   This dwarf is no other than Mimmy, the brother of Alberic, the same who made for him the magic helmet.   His aim in life is to gain possession of the helmet, the ring, and the treasure, and through them to obtain that Plutonic mastery of the world under the beginnings of which he himself writhed during Alberic's brief reign. Mimmy is a blinking, shambling, ancient creature, too weak and timid to dream of taking arms himself to despoil Fafnir, who still, transformed to a monstrous serpent, broods on the gold in a hole in the rocks.   Mimmy needs the help of a hero for that; and he has craft enough to know that it is quite possible, and indeed much in the ordinary way of the world, for senile avarice and craft to set youth and bravery to work to win empire for it.   He knows the pedigree of the child left on his hands, and nurses it to manhood with great care.

His pains are too well rewarded for his comfort.   The boy Siegfried, having no god to instruct him in the art of unhappiness, inherits none of his father's ill luck, and all his father's hardihood.   The fear against which Siegmund set his face like flint, and the woe which he wore down, are unknown to the son.   The father was faithful and grateful:

43

the son knows no law but his own humor; detests the ugly dwarf who has nursed him; chafes furiously under his claims for some return for his tender care; and is, in short, a totally unmoral person, a born anarchist, the ideal of Bakoonin, an anticipation of the "overman" of Nietzsche. He is enormously strong, full of life and fun, dangerous and destructive to what he dislikes, and affectionate to what he likes; so that it is fortunate that his likes and dislikes are sane and healthy. Altogether an inspiriting young forester, a son of the morning, in whom the heroic race has come out into the sunshine from the clouds of his grandfather's majestic entanglements with law, and the night of his father's tragic struggle with it.

The First Act

Mimmy's smithy is a cave, in which he hides from the light like the eyeless fish of the American caverns. Before the curtain rises the music already tells us that we are groping in darkness. When it does rise Mimmy is in difficulties. He is trying to make a sword for his nursling, who is now big enough to take the field against Fafnir. Mimmy can make mischievous swords; but it is not with dwarf-made weapons that heroic man will hew the way of his own will through religions and governments and plutoc-racies and all the other devices of the kingdom of the fears of the unheroic. As fast as Mimmy makes swords, Siegfried Bakoonin smashes them, and then takes the poor old swordsmith by the scruff of the neck and chastises him wrathfully. The particular day on which the curtain rises begins with one of these trying domestic incidents. Mimmy has just done his best with a new sword of surpassing excel-lence. Siegfried returns home in rare spirits with a wild bear, to the extreme terror of the wretched dwarf. When the bear is dismissed, the new sword is produced. It is

promptly smashed, as usual, with, also, the usual effects on
the temper of Siegfried, who is quite boundless in his
criticisms of the smith's boasted skill, and declares that he
would smash the sword's maker too if he were not too
disgusting to be handled.

Mimmy falls back on his stock defence: a string of maudlin
reminders of the care with which he has nursed the little boy
into manhood. Siegfried replies candidly that the strangest
thing about all this care is that instead of making him
grateful, it inspires him with a lively desire to wring the
dwarf's neck. Only, he admits that he always comes back
to his Mimmy, though he loathes him more than any living
thing in the forest. On this admission the dwarf attempts to
build a theory of filial instinct. He explains that he is
Siegfried's father, and that this is why Siegfried cannot do
without him. But Siegfried has learned from his forest
companions, the birds and foxes and wolves, that mothers as
well as fathers go to the making of children. Mimmy, on
the desperate ground that man is neither bird nor fox,
declares that he is Siegfried's father and mother both. He
is promptly denounced as a filthy liar, because the birds and
foxes are exactly like their parents, whereas Siegfried,
having often watched his own image in the water, can testify
that he is no more like Mimmy than a toad is like a trout.
Then, to place the conversation on a plane of entire frankness,
he throttles Mimmy until he is speechless. When the dwarf
recovers, he is so daunted that he tells Siegfried the truth
about his birth, and for testimony thereof produces the pieces
of the sword that broke upon Wotan's spear. Siegfried
instantly orders him to repair the sword on pain of an
unmerciful thrashing, and rushes off into the forest, rejoicing
in the discovery that he is no kin to Mimmy's, and need have
no more to do with him when the sword is mended.

Poor Mimmy is now in a worse plight than ever; for he has
long ago found that the sword utterly defies his skill: the steel

will yield neither to his hammer nor to his furnace. Just
then there walks into his cave a Wanderer, in a blue mantle,
spear in hand, with one eye concealed by the brim of his
wide hat. Mimmy, not by nature hospitable, tries to drive
him away; but the Wanderer announces himself as a wise
man, who can tell his host, in emergency, what it most
concerns him to know. Mimmy, taking this offer in high
dudgeon, because it implies that his visitor's wits are better
than his own, offers to tell the wise one something that *he* does
not know: to wit, the way to the door. The imperturbable
Wanderer's reply is to sit down and challenge the dwarf to a
trial of wit. He wagers his head against Mimmy's that he
will answer any three questions the dwarf can put to him.

Now here were Mimmy's opportunity, had he only the
wit to ask what he wants to know, instead of pretending to
know everything already. It is above all things needful to
him at this moment to find out how that sword can be
mended; and there has just dropped in upon him in his need
the one person who can tell him. In such circumstances a
wise man would hasten to show to his visitor his three deepest
ignorances, and ask him to dispel them. The dwarf, being a
crafty fool, desiring only to detect ignorance in his guest,
asks him for information on the three points on which he is
proudest of being thoroughly well instructed himself. His
three questions are, Who dwell under the earth? Who
dwell on the earth? and Who dwell in the cloudy heights
above? The Wanderer, in reply, tells him of the dwarfs
and of Alberic; of the earth, and the giants Fasolt and
Fafnir; of the gods and of Wotan: himself, as Mimmy now
recognizes with awe.

Next, it is Mimmy's turn to face three questions. What
is that race, dearest to Wotan, against which Wotan has
nevertheless done his worst? Mimmy can answer that: he
knows the Volsungs, the race of heroes born of Wotan's
infidelities to Fricka, and can tell the Wanderer the whole

story of the twins and their son Siegfried. Wotan compliments him on his knowledge, and asks further with what
sword Siegfried will slay Fafnir? Mimmy can answer that
too: he has the whole history of the sword at his fingers' ends.
Wotan hails him as the knowingest of the knowing, and then
hurls at him the question he should himself have asked: Who
will mend the sword? Mimmy, his head forfeited, confesses
with loud lamentations that he cannot answer. The
Wanderer reads him an appropriate little lecture on the
folly of being too clever to ask what he wants to know, and
informs him that a smith to whom fear is unknown will mend
Nothung. To this smith he leaves the forfeited head of his
host, and wanders off into the forest. Then Mimmy's nerves
give way completely. He shakes like a man in delirium
tremens, and has a horrible nightmare, in the supreme
convulsion of which Siegfried, returning from the forest,
presently finds him.

A curious and amusing conversation follows. Siegfried
himself does not know fear, and is impatient to acquire it
as an accomplishment. Mimmy is all fear: the world for
him is a phantasmagoria of terrors. It is not that he is
afraid of being eaten by bears in the forest, or of burning his
fingers in the forge fire. A lively objection to being destroyed
or maimed does not make a man a coward: on the contrary,
it is the beginning of a brave man's wisdom. But in
Mimmy, fear is not the effect of danger: it is a natural
quality of him which no security can allay. He is like many
a poor newspaper editor, who dares not print the truth,
however simple, even when it is obvious to himself and all
his readers. Not that anything unpleasant would happen
to him if he did—not, indeed, that he could fail to become a
distinguished and influential leader of opinion by fearlessly
pursuing such a course, but solely because he lives in a
world of imaginary terrors, rooted in a modest and gentle-
manly mistrust of his own strength and worth, and

consequently of the value of his opinion. Just so is Mimmy afraid of anything that can do him any good, especially of the light and the fresh air. He is also convinced that anybody who is not sufficiently steeped in fear to be constantly on his guard, must perish immediately on his first sally into the world. To preserve Siegfried for the enterprise to which he has destined him he makes a grotesque attempt to teach him fear. He appeals to his experience of the terrors of the forest, of its dark places, of its threatening noises, its stealthy ambushes, its sinister flickering lights, its heart-tightening ecstasies of dread.

All this has no other effect than to fill Siegfried with wonder and curiosity; for the forest is a place of delight for him. He is as eager to experience Mimmy's terrors as a schoolboy to feel what an electric shock is like. Then Mimmy has the happy idea of describing Fafnir to him as a likely person to give him an exemplary fright. Siegfried jumps at the idea, and, since Mimmy cannot mend the sword for him, proposes to set to work then and there to mend it for himself. Mimmy shakes his head, and bids him see now how his youthful laziness and forwardness have found him out—how he would not learn the smith's craft from Professor Mimmy, and therefore does not know how even to begin mending the sword. Siegfried Bakoonin's retort is simple and crushing. He points out that the net result of Mimmy's academic skill is that he can neither make a decent sword himself nor even set one to rights when it is damaged. Reckless of the remonstrances of the scandalized professor, he seizes a file, and in a few moments utterly destroys the fragments of the sword by rasping them into a heap of steel filings. Then he puts the filings into a crucible; buries it in the coals; and sets to at the bellows with the shouting exultation of the anarchist who destroys only to clear the ground for creation. When the steel is melted he runs it into a mould; and lo! a sword-blade in the rough.

Mimmy, amazed at the success of this violation of all the rules of his craft, hails Siegfried as the mightiest of smiths, professing himself barely worthy to be his cook and scullion; and forthwith proceeds to poison some soup for him so that he may murder him safely when Fafnir is slain. Meanwhile Siegfried forges and tempers and hammers and rivets, uproariously singing the while as nonsensically as the Rhine daughters themselves. Finally he assails the anvil on which Mimmy's swords have been shattered, and cleaves it with a mighty stroke of the newly forged Nothung.

The Second Act

In the darkest hour before the dawn of that night, we find ourselves before the cave of Fafnir; and there we find Alberic, who can find nothing better to do with himself than to watch the haunt of the dragon, and eat his heart out in vain longing for the gold and the ring. The wretched Fafnir, once an honest giant, can only make himself terrible enough to keep his gold by remaining a venomous reptile. Why he should not become an honest giant again, and clear out of his cavern, leaving the gold and the ring and the rest of it for anyone fool enough to take them at such a price, is the first question that would occur to anyone except a civilized man, who would be too accustomed to that sort of mania to be at all surprised at it.

To Alberic in the night comes the Wanderer, whom the dwarf, recognizing his despoiler of old, abuses as a shameless thief, taunting him with the helpless way in which all his boasted power is tied up with the laws and bargains recorded on the haft of his spear, which, says Alberic truly, would crumble like chaff in his hands if he dared use it for his own real ends. Wotan, having already had to kill his own son with it, knows that very well; but it troubles him no more; for he is now at last rising to abhorrence of his own artificial power, and looking to the coming hero, not for its consolidation but its destruction. When Alberic breaks out again with his still unquenched hope of one day destroying the gods and ruling the world through the ring, Wotan is no longer shocked. He tells Alberic that Brother Mime approaches with a hero whom Godhead can neither help nor hinder. Alberic may try his luck against him without disturbance from Valhalla. Perhaps, he suggests, if Alberic warns Fafnir, and offers to deal with the hero for him, Fafnir may give him the ring. They accordingly wake up the dragon, who condescends to enter into bellowing conversation, but is proof against their proposition, strong in the magic of property. "I have and hold," he says: "leave me to sleep." Wotan, with a wise laugh, turns to Alberic. "That shot missed," he says: "no use abusing me for it. And now let me tell you one thing. All things happen according to their nature; and *you* can't alter them." And so he leaves him. Alberic, raging with the sense that his old enemy has been laughing at him, and yet prophetically convinced that the last word will not be with the god, hides himself as the day breaks, and his brother approaches with Siegfried.

Mimmy makes a final attempt to frighten Siegfried by discoursing of the dragon's terrible jaws, poisonous breath, corrosive spittle, and deadly, stinging tail. Siegfried is not interested in the tail: he wants to know whether the dragon has a heart, being confident of his ability to stick Nothung into it if it exists. Reassured on this point, he drives Mimmy away, and stretches himself under the trees, listening to the morning chatter of the birds. One of them has a great deal to say to him; but he cannot understand it; and after vainly trying to carry on the conversation with a reed which he cuts, he takes to entertaining the bird with tunes on his horn, asking it to send him a loving mate such as all the other creatures of the forest have. His tunes wake up the dragon; and Siegfried makes merry over the grim mate the bird has sent him. Fafnir is highly scandalized by the irreverence of the young Bakoonin. He loses his temper; fights; and is forthwith slain, to his own great astonishment. In such conflicts one learns to interpret the messages of Nature a little. When Siegfried, stung by the dragon's vitriolic blood, pops his finger into his mouth and tastes it, he understands what the bird is saying to him, and, instructed by it concerning the treasures within his reach, goes into the cave to secure the gold, the ring and the wishing cap. Then Mimmy returns, and is confronted by Alberic. The two quarrel furiously over the sharing of the booty they have not yet secured, until Siegfried comes from the cave with the ring and the helmet, not much impressed by the heap of gold, and disappointed because he has not yet learned to fear.

He has, however, learnt to read the thoughts of such a creature as poor Mimmy, who, intending to overwhelm him with flattery and fondness, only succeeds in making such a self-revelation of murderous envy that Siegfried smites him with Nothung and slays him, to the keen satisfaction of the hidden Alberic. Caring nothing for the gold, which he leaves to the care of the slain; disappointed in his fancy for learning fear; and longing for a mate, he casts himself wearily down, and again appeals to his friend the bird, who tells him of a woman sleeping on a mountain peak within a fortress of fire that only the fearless can penetrate. Siegfried is up in a moment with all the tumult of spring in his veins, and follows the flight of the bird as it pilots him to the fiery mountain.

The Third Act

To the root of the mountain comes also the Wanderer, now nearing his doom. He calls up the First Mother from the depths of the earth, and begs counsel from her. She

bids him confer with the Norns (the Fates).   But they are of
no use to him: what he seeks is some foreknowledge of the
way of the Will in its perpetual strife with these helpless
Fates who can only spin the net of circumstance and environment round the feet of men.   Why not, says Erda then, go
to the daughter I bore you, and take counsel with her?   He
has to explain how he has cut himself off from her, and set
the fires of Loki between the world and her counsel.   In
that case the First Mother cannot help him: such a separation
is part of the bewilderment that is ever the first outcome of
her eternal work of thrusting the life energy of the world to
higher and higher organization.   She can show him no way
of escape from the destruction he foresees.   Then from the
innermost of him breaks the confession that he rejoices in his
doom, and now himself exults in passing away with all his
ordinances and alliances, with the spear-sceptre which he
has only wielded on condition of slaying his dearest children
with it, with the kingdom, the power and the glory which
will never again boast themselves as "world without end."
And so he dismisses Erda to her sleep in the heart of the
earth as the forest bird draws near, piloting the slain son's
son to his goal.

   Now it is an excellent thing to triumph in the victory of the
new order and the passing away of the old; but if you happen
to be part of the old order yourself, you must none the less
fight for your life. It seems hardly possible that the British
army at the battle of Waterloo did not include at least one
Englishman intelligent enough to hope, for the sake of his
country and humanity, that Napoleon might defeat the allied
sovereigns; but such an Englishman would kill a French
cuirassier rather than be killed by him just as energetically
as the silliest soldier ever encouraged, by people who ought
to know better, to call his ignorance, ferocity and folly,
patriotism and duty. Outworn life may have become mere
error; but it still claims the right to die a natural death, and

will raise its hand against the millennium itself in self-
defence if it tries to come by the short cut of murder. Wotan
finds this out when he comes face to face with Siegfried,
who is brought to a standstill at the foot of the mountain
by the disappearance of the bird. Meeting the Wanderer
there, he asks him the way to the mountain where a woman
sleeps surrounded by fire. The Wanderer questions him,
and extracts his story from him, breaking into fatherly
delight when Siegfried, describing the mending of the sword,
remarks that all hc kncw about thc busincss was that thc
broken bits of Nothung would be of no use to him unless he
made a new sword out of them right over again from the
beginning. But the Wanderer's interest is by no means
reciprocated by Siegfried. His majesty and elderly dignity
are thrown away on the young anarchist, who, unwilling to
waste time talking, bluntly bids him either show him the way
to the mountain, or else "shut his muzzle." Wotan is a
little hurt. "Patience, my lad," he says: "if I seem old to
you, you should treat me with respect." "That would be a
precious notion," says Siegfried. "All my life long I was
bothered and hampered by an old man until I swept him
out of my way. I will sweep you in the same fashion if you
don't let me pass. Why do you wear such a big hat; and
what has happened to one of your eyes? was it knocked out
by somebody whose way you obstructed?" To which
Wotan replies allegorically that the eye that is gone—the
eye that his marriage with Fricka cost him—is now looking
at him out of Siegfried's head. At this, Siegfried gives up
the Wanderer as a lunatic, and renews his threats of personal
violence. Then Wotan throws off the mask of the Wanderer;
uplifts the world-governing spear; and puts forth all his
divine awe and grandeur as the guardian of the mountain,
round the crest of which the fires of Loki now break into a
red background for the majesty of the god. But all this is
lost on Siegfried Bakoonin. "Aha!" he cries, as the spear is

levelled against his breast: "I have found my father's foe"; and the spear falls in two pieces under the stroke of Nothung. "Up then," says Wotan: "I cannot withhold you," and disappears forever from the eye of man. The fires roll down the mountain; but Siegfried goes at them as exultantly as he went at the forging of the sword or the heart of the dragon, and shoulders his way through them, joyously sounding his horn to the accompaniment of their crackling and seething. And never a hair of his head is singed. Those frightful flames which have scared mankind for centuries from the Truth, have not heat enough in them to make a child shut its eyes. They are mere phantasmagoria, highly creditable to Loki's imaginative stage-management; but nothing ever has perished or will perish eternally in them except the Churches which have been so poor and faithless as to trade for their power on the lies of a romancer.

BACK TO OPERA AGAIN

And now, O Nibelungen Spectator, pluck up; for all allegories come to an end somewhere; and the hour of your release from these explanations is at hand. The rest of what you are going to see is opera, and nothing but opera. Before many bars have been played, Siegfried and the wakened Brynhild, newly become tenor and soprano, will sing a concerted cadenza; plunge on from that to a magnificent love duet; and end with a precipitous *allegro a cappella*, driven headlong to its end by the impetuous semiquaver triplets of the famous finales to the first act of *Don Giovanni* or the coda to the *Leonore* overture, with a specifically contrapuntal theme, *points d'orgue*, and a high C for the soprano all complete.

What is more, the work which follows, entitled *Night Falls on the Gods*, is a thorough grand opera. In it you shall see what you have so far missed, the opera chorus in full parade on the stage, not presuming to interfere with the prima donna as she sings her death song over the footlights. Nay, that chorus will have its own chance when it first appears, with a good roaring strain in C major, not, after all, so very different from, or at all less absurd than the choruses of courtiers in *La Favorita* or "Per te d'immenso guibilo" in *Lucia*. The harmony is no doubt a little developed, Wagner augmenting his fifths with a G sharp where Donizetti would have put his fingers in his ears and screamed for G natural. But it is an opera chorus all the same; and along with it we have theatrical grandiosities that recall Meyerbeer and Verdi: *pezzi d'insieme* for all the principals in a row, vengeful conjurations for trios of them, romantic death song for the tenor: in short, all manner of operatic conventions.

Now it is probable that some of us will have been so talked by the more superstitious Bayreuth pilgrims into regarding *Die Götterdämmerung* as the mighty climax to a mighty epic, more Wagnerian than all the other three sections put together, as not to dare notice this startling atavism, especially if we find the trio-conjurations more exhilarating than the metaphysical discourses of Wotan in the three true music dramas of *The Ring*. There is, however, no real atavism involved. *Die Götterdämmerung*, though the last of the *Ring* dramas in order of performance, was the first in order of conception, and was indeed the root from which all the others sprang.

The history of the matter is as follows. All Wagner's works prior to *The Ring* are operas. The last of them, *Lohengrin*, is perhaps the best known of modern operas. As performed in its entirety at Bayreuth, it is even more operatic than it appears at Covent Garden, because it happens that its most old-fashioned features, notably some of the big set concerted pieces for principals and chorus (*pezzi d'insieme* as I have called them above), are harder to perform than the more modern and characteristically Wagnerian sections, and for that reason were cut out in preparing the abbreviated fashionable version.   Thus *Lohengrin* came upon the ordinary operatic stage as a more advanced departure from current operatic models than its composer had made it.   Still, it is unmistakably an opera, with chorus, concerted pieces, grand finales, and a heroine who, if she does not sing florid variations with flute obbligato, is none the less a very perceptible prima donna.   In everything but musical technique the change from *Lohengrin* to *The Rhine Gold* is quite revolutionary.

The explanation is that *Night Falls on the Gods* came in between them, although its music was not finished until twenty years after that of *The Rhine Gold*, and thus belongs to a later and more masterful phase of Wagner's harmonic style.   It first came into Wagner's head as an opera to be entitled *Siegfried's Death*, founded on the old Niblung Sagas, which offered to Wagner the same material for an effective theatrical tragedy as they did to Ibsen.   Ibsen's *Vikings in Helgeland* is, in kind, what *Siegfried's Death* was originally intended to be: that is, a heroic piece for the theatre, without the metaphysical or allegorical complications of *The Ring*.   Indeed, the ultimate catastrophe of the Saga cannot by any perversion of ingenuity be adapted to the perfectly clear allegorical design of *The Rhine Gold*, *The Valkyrie*, and *Siegfried*.

SIEGFRIED AS
PROTESTANT

The philosophically fertile element in the original project of *Siegfried's Death* was the conception of Siegfried himself as a type of the healthy man raised to perfect confidence in his own impulses by an intense and joyous vitality which is above fear, sickliness of conscience, malice, and the makeshifts and moral crutches of law and order which accompany them. Such a character appears extraordinarily fascinating and exhilarating to our guilty and conscience-ridden generations, however little they may understand him. The world has always delighted in the man who is delivered from conscience. From Punch and Don Juan down to Robert Macaire, Jeremy Diddler and the pantomime clown, he has always drawn large audiences; but hitherto he has been decorously given to the devil at the end. Indeed eternal punishment is sometimes deemed too high a compliment to his nature. When the late Lord Lytton, in his *Strange Story*, introduced a character personifying the joyousness of intense vitality, he felt bound to deny him the immortal soul which was at that time conceded even to the humblest characters in fiction, and to accept mischievousness, cruelty, and utter incapacity for sympathy as the inevitable consequence of his magnificent bodily and mental health.

In short, though men felt all the charm of abounding life
and abandonment to its impulses, they dared not, in their
deep self-mistrust, conceive it otherwise than as a force
making for evil—one which must lead to universal ruin
unless checked and literally mortified by self-renunciation
in obedience to superhuman guidance, or at least to some
reasoned system of morals.   When it became apparent to the
cleverest of them that no such superhuman guidance existed,
and that their secularist systems had all the fictitiousness of
"revelation" without its poetry, there was no escaping the
conclusion that all the good that man had done must be put
down to his arbitrary will as well as all the evil he had done;
and it was also obvious that if progress were a reality, his
beneficent impulses must be gaining on his destructive ones.
It was under the influence of these ideas that we began to
hear about the joy of life where we had formerly heard
about the grace of God or the Age of Reason, and that the
boldest spirits began to raise the question whether churches
and laws and the like were not doing a great deal more harm
than good by their action in limiting the freedom of the
human will.   Four hundred years ago, when belief in God
and in revelation was general throughout Europe, a similar
wave of thought led the strongest-hearted peoples to affirm
that every man's private judgment was a more trustworthy
interpreter of God and revelation than the Church.   This
was called Protestantism; and though the Protestants were
not strong enough for their creed, and soon set up a Church
of their own, yet the movement, on the whole, has justified
the direction it took.   Nowadays the supernatural element
in Protestantism has perished; and if every man's private
judgment is still to be justified as the most trustworthy
interpreter of the will of Humanity (which is not a more
extreme proposition than the old one about the will of God)
Protestantism must take a fresh step in advance, and
become Anarchism.   Which it has accordingly done,

Anarchism being one of the notable new creeds of the eighteenth and nineteenth centuries.

The weak place which experience finds out in the Anarchist theory is its reliance on the progress already achieved by "Man." There is no such thing as Man in the world: what we have to deal with is a multitude of men, some of them great rascals, some of them great statesmen, others both, with a vast majority capable of managing their personal affairs, but not of comprehending social organization, or grappling with the problems created by their association in enormous numbers. If "Man" means this majority, then "Man" has made no progress: he has, on the contrary, resisted it. He will not even pay the cost of existing institutions: the requisite money has to be filched from him by "indirect taxation." Such people, like Wagner's giants, must be governed by laws; and their assent to such government must be secured by deliberately filling them with prejudices and practising on their imaginations by pageantry and artificial eminences and dignities. The government is of course established by the few who are capable of government, though, its mechanism once complete, it may be, and generally is, carried on unintelligently by people who are incapable of it, the capable people repairing it from time to time when it gets too far behind the continuous advance or decay of civilization. All these capable people are thus in the position of Wotan, forced to maintain as sacred, and themselves submit to, laws which they privately know to be obsolescent makeshifts, and to affect the deepest veneration for creeds and ideals which they ridicule among themselves with cynical scepticism. No individual Siegfried can rescue them from this bondage and hypocrisy; in fact, the individual Siegfried has come often enough, only to find himself confronted with the alternative of governing those who are not Siegfrieds or risking destruction at their hands. And this dilemma will persist until Wotan's inspiration comes to our governors, and they see that their business is not the devising of laws and institutions to prop up the weaknesses of mobs and secure the survival of the unfittest, but the breeding of men whose wills and intelligences may be depended on to produce spontaneously the social well-being our clumsy laws now aim at and miss. The majority of men at present in Europe have no business to be alive; and no serious progress will be made until we address ourselves earnestly and scientifically to the task of producing trustworthy human material for society. In short, it is necessary to breed a race of men in whom the life-giving impulses predominate, before the New Protestantism becomes politically practicable.[1]

The most inevitable dramatic conception, then, of the nineteenth century, is that of a perfectly naïve hero upsetting religion, law and order in all directions, and establishing in their place the unfettered action of Humanity doing exactly what it likes, and producing order instead of confusion thereby because it likes to do what is necessary for the good of the race. This conception, already incipient in Adam Smith's *Wealth of Nations*, was certain at last to reach some great artist, and be embodied by him in a masterpiece. It was also certain that if that master happened to be a German, he should take delight in describing his hero as the Freewiller of Necessity, thereby beyond measure exasperating Englishmen with a congenital incapacity for metaphysics.

PANACEA QUACKERY, OTHERWISE IDEALISM

Unfortunately, human enlightenment does not progress by nicer and nicer adjustments, but by violent corrective

[1] The necessity for breeding the governing class from a selected stock has always been recognized by Aristocrats, however erroneous their methods of selection. We have changed our system from Aristocracy to Democracy with-

reactions which invariably send us clean over our saddle and would bring us to the ground on the other side if the next reaction did not send us back again with equally excessive zeal. Ecclesiasticism and Constitutionalism send us one way, Protestantism and Anarchism the other; Order rescues us from confusion and lands us in Tyranny; Liberty then saves the situation and is presently found to be as great a nuisance as Despotism. A scientifically balanced application of these forces, theoretically possible, is practically incompatible with human passion. Besides, we have the same weakness in morals as in medicine: we cannot be cured of running after panaceas, or, as they are called in the sphere of morals, ideals. One generation sets up duty, renunciation, self-sacrifice as a panacea. The next generation, especially the women, wake up at the age of forty or thereabouts to the fact that their lives have been wasted in the worship of this ideal, and, what is still more aggravating, that the elders who imposed it on them did so in a fit of satiety with their own experiments in the other direction. Then that defrauded generation foams at the mouth at the very mention of duty, and sets up the alternative panacea of love, their deprivation of which seems to them to have been the most cruel and mischievous feature of their slavery to duty. It is useless to warn them that this reaction, if prescribed as a panacea, will prove as great a failure as all the other reactions have done; for they do not recognize its identity with any reaction that ever occurred before. Take for instance the hackneyed historic example of the austerity of the Commonwealth being followed by the licence of the Restoration. You cannot persuade any moral enthusiast to accept this as a pure oscillation from action to reaction. If he is a Puritan he looks upon the Restoration as a national

out considering that we were at the same time changing, as regards our governing class, from Selection to Promiscuity. Those who have taken a practical part in modern politics best know how farcical the result is.

disaster: if he is an artist he regards it as the salvation of the
country from gloom, devil worship and starvation of the
affections.   The Puritan is ready to try the Commonwealth
again with a few modern improvements: the Amateur is
equally ready to try the Restoration with modern enlighten-
ments.   And so for the present we must be content to pro-
ceed by reactions, hoping that each will establish some
permanently practical and beneficial reform or moral habit
that will survive the correction of its excesses by the next
reaction.

DRAMATIC ORIGIN OF WOTAN

We can now see how a single drama in which Wotan does
not appear, and of which Siegfried is the hero, expanded
itself into a great fourfold drama of which Wotan is the hero.
You cannot dramatize a reaction by personifying the reacting
force only, any more than Archimedes could lift the world
without a fulcrum for his lever.   You must also personify
the established power against which the new force is reacting;
and in the conflict between them you get your drama,
conflict being the essential ingredient in all drama.   Siegfried, as the hero of *Die Götterdämmerung*, is only the *primo
tenore robusto* of an opera book, deferring his death, after he
has been stabbed in the last act, to sing rapturous love strains
to the heroine exactly like Edgardo in Donizetti's *Lucia*.   In
order to make him intelligible in the wider significance which
his joyous, fearless, conscienceless heroism soon assumed in
Wagner's imagination, it was necessary to provide him with
a much vaster dramatic antagonist than the operatic villain
Hagen.   Hence Wagner had to create Wotan as the anvil
for Siegfried's hammer; and since there was no room for
Wotan in the original opera book, Wagner had to work
back to a preliminary drama reaching primarily to the very

beginnings of human society. And since, on this world-embracing scale, it was clear that Siegfried must come into conflict with many baser and stupider forces than those lofty ones of supernatural religion and political constitutionalism typified by Wotan and his wife Fricka, these minor antagonists had to be dramatized also in the persons of Alberic, Mime, Fafnir, Loki, and the rest. None of these appear in *Night Falls on the Gods* save Alberic, whose weird dream-colloquy with Hagen, effective as it is, is as purely theatrical as the scene of the Ghost in *Hamlet*, or the statue in *Don Giovanni*. Cut the conference of the Norns and the visit of Valtrauta to Brynhild out of *Night Falls on the Gods*, and the drama remains coherent and complete without them. Retain them, and the play becomes connected by conversational references with the three music dramas; but the connection establishes no philosophic coherence, no real identity between the operatic Brynhild of the Gibichung episode (presently to be related) and the daughter of Wotan and the First Mother.

THE LOVE PANACEA

We shall now find that at the point where *The Ring* changes from music drama into opera, it also ceases to be philosophic, and becomes didactic. The philosophic part is a dramatic symbol of the world as Wagner observed it. In the didactic part the philosophy degenerates into the prescription of a romantic nostrum for all human ills. Wagner, only mortal, after all, succumbed to the panacea mania when his philosophy was exhausted, like any of the rest of us.

The panacea is by no means an original one. Wagner was anticipated in the year 1819 by a young country gentleman from Sussex named Shelley, in a work of extraordinary artistic power and splendor. *Prometheus Unbound* is an English attempt at a *Ring*; and when it is taken into account that the author was only 27, whereas Wagner was 40 when he completed the poem of *The Ring*, our vulgar patriotism may find an envious satisfaction in insisting upon the comparison. Both works set forth the same conflict between humanity and its gods and governments, issuing in the redemption of man from their tyranny by the growth of his will into perfect strength and self-confidence; and both finish by a lapse into panacea-mongering didacticism by the holding up of Love as the remedy for all evils and the solvent of all social difficulties.

The differences between *Prometheus Unbound* and *The Ring* are as interesting as the likenesses. Shelley, caught in the pugnacity of his youth and the first impetuosity of his prodigious artistic power by the first fierce attack of the New Reformation, gave no quarter to the antagonist of his hero. His Wotan, whom he calls Jupiter, is the almighty fiend into whom the Englishman's God had degenerated during two centuries of ignorant Bible worship and shameless commercialism. He is Alberic, Fafnir, Loki and the ambitious side of Wotan all rolled into one melodramatic demon who is finally torn from his throne and hurled shrieking into the abyss by a spirit representing that conception of Eternal Law which has been replaced since by the conception of Evolution. Wagner, an older, more experienced man than the Shelley of 1819, understood Wotan and pardoned him, separating him tenderly from all the compromising alliances to which Shelley fiercely held him; making the truth and heroism which overthrow him the children of his inmost heart; and representing him as finally acquiescing in and working for his own supersession and annihilation. Shelley, in his later works, is seen progressing towards the same tolerance, justice, and humility of spirit, as he advanced towards the middle age he never reached.

But there is no progress from Shelley to Wagner as regards the panacea, except that in Wagner there is a certain shadow of night and death come on it; nay, even a clear opinion that the supreme good of love is that it so completely satisfies the desire for life, that after it the Will to Live ceases to trouble us, and we are at last content to achieve the highest happiness of death.

This reduction of the panacea to absurdity was not forced upon Shelley, because the love which acts as a universal solvent in his *Prometheus Unbound* is a sentiment of affectionate benevolence which has nothing to do with sexual passion. It might, and in fact does, exist in the absence of any sexual interest whatever. The words mercy and kindness connote it less ambiguously than the word love. But Wagner sought always for some point of contact between his ideas and the physical senses, so that people might not only think or imagine them in the eighteenth-century fashion, but see them on the stage, hear them from the orchestra, and feel them through the infection of passionate emotion. Dr. Johnson kicking the stone to confute Berkeley is not more bent on common-sense concreteness than Wagner: on all occasions he insists on the need for sensuous apprehension to give reality to abstract comprehension, maintaining, in fact, that reality has no other meaning. Now he could apply this process to poetic love only by following it back to its alleged origin in sexual passion, the emotional phenomena of which he has expressed in music with a frankness and forcible naturalism which would possibly have scandalized Shelley. The love duet in the first act of *The Valkyrie* is brought to a point at which the conventions of our society demand the precipitate fall of the curtain; whilst the prelude to *Tristan and Isolde* is such an astonishingly intense and faithful translation into music of the emotions which accompany the union of a pair of lovers, that it is questionable whether the great popularity of this piece at our orchestral concerts really means that our audiences are entirely catholic in their respect for life in all its beneficently creative functions, or whether they simply enjoy the music without understanding it.

But however offensive and inhuman may be the superstition which brands such exaltations of natural passion as shameful and indecorous, there is at least as much common sense in disparaging love as in setting it up as a panacea. Even the mercy and lovingkindness of Shelley do not hold good as a universal law of conduct: Shelley himself makes extremely short work of Jupiter, just as Siegfried does of Fafnir, Mime, and Wotan; and the fact that Prometheus is saved from doing the destructive part of his work by the intervention of that very nebulous personification of Eternity called Demogorgon, does not in the least save the situation, because, flatly, there is no such person as Demogorgon, and if Prometheus does not pull down Jupiter himself, no one else will. It would be exasperating, if it were not so funny, to see these poets leading their heroes through blood and destruction to the conclusion that, as Browning's David puts it (David of all people!), "All's Love; yet all's Law."

Certainly it is clear enough that such love as that implied by Siegfried's first taste of fear as he cuts through the mailed coat of the sleeping figure on the mountain, and discovers that it is a woman; by her fierce revolt against being touched by him when his terror gives way to ardor; by his manly transports of victory; and by the womanly mixture of rapture and horror with which she abandons herself to the passion which has seized on them both, is an experience which it is much better, like the vast majority of us, never to have passed through, than to allow it to play more than a recreative holiday part in our lives. It did not play a very large part in Wagner's own laborious life, and does not occupy more than two scenes of *The Ring*. *Tristan and Isolde*, wholly devoted to it, is a poem of destruction and death. *The Mastersingers*, a work full of health, fun and happiness, contains not a single bar of love music that can be described as passionate: the hero of it is a widower who cobbles shoes, writes verses, and contents himself with looking on at the sweethearting of his customers. *Parsifal* makes an end of it altogether. The truth is that the love panacea in *Night Falls on the Gods* and in the last act of *Siegfried* is a survival of the first crude operatic conception of the story, modified by an anticipation of Wagner's later, though not latest, conception of love as the fulfiller of our Will to Live and consequently our reconciler to night and death.

NOT LOVE, BUT LIFE

The only faith which any reasonable disciple can gain from *The Ring* is not in love, but in life itself as a tireless power which is continually driving onward and upward—not, please observe, being beckoned or drawn by *Das Ewig Weibliche* or any other external sentimentality, but growing from within, by its own inexplicable energy, into ever higher and higher forms of organization, the strengths and the needs of which are continually superseding the institutions which were made to fit our former requirements. When your Bakoonins call out for the demolition of all these venerable institutions, there is no need to fly into a panic and lock them up in prison whilst your parliament is bit by bit doing exactly what they advised you to do. When your Siegfrieds melt down the old weapons into new ones, and with disrespectful words chop in twain the antiquated constable's staves in the hands of their elders, the end of the world is no nearer than it was before. If human nature, which is the highest organization of life reached on this planet, is really degenerating, then human society will decay; and no panic-begotten penal measures can possibly save it: we must, like Prometheus, set to work to make new men instead of vainly torturing old ones. On the other hand, if the energy of life is still carrying human nature to higher and higher levels, then the more young people shock their elders and deride and discard their pet institutions, the better for the hopes of the world, since the apparent growth of anarchy is only the measure of the rate of improvement. History, as far as we are capable of history (which is not saying much as yet), shows that all changes from crudity of social organization to complexity, and from mechanical agencies in government to living ones, seem anarchic at first sight. No doubt it is natural to a snail to think that any evolution which threatens to do away with shells will result in general death from exposure. Nevertheless, the most elaborately housed beings today are born not only without houses on their backs but without even fur or feathers to clothe them.

ANARCHISM NO PANACEA

One word of warning to those who may find themselves attracted by Siegfried's Anarchism, or, if they prefer a term with more respectable associations, his neo-Protestantism. Anarchism, as a panacea, is just as hopeless as any other panacea, and will still be so even if we breed a race of perfectly benevolent men. It is true that in the sphere of thought, Anarchism is an inevitable condition of progressive evolution. A nation without Freethinkers—that is, without intellectual Anarchists—will share the fate of China. It is also true that our criminal law, based on a conception of crime and punishment which is nothing but our vindictiveness and cruelty in a virtuous disguise, is an unmitigated and abominable nuisance, bound to be beaten out of us finally

by the mere weight of our experience of its evil and useless-
ness. But it will not be replaced by anarchy. Applied to
the industrial or political machinery of modern society,
anarchy must always reduce itself speedily to absurdity.
Even the modified form of anarchy on which modern
civilization is based: that is, the abandonment of industry,
in the name of individual liberty, to the upshot of competi-
tion for personal gain between private capitalists, is a
disastrous failure, and is, by the mere necessities of the case,
giving way to ordered Socialism. For the economic
rationale of this, I must refer disciples of Siegfried to a tract
from my hand published by the Fabian Society and entitled
The Impossibilities of Anarchism, which explains why, owing
to the physical constitution of our globe, society cannot
effectively organize the production of its food, clothes and
housing, nor distribute them fairly and economically on
any anarchic plan: nay, that without concerting our social
action to a much higher degree than we do at present we
can never get rid of the wasteful and iniquitous welter of a
little riches and a great deal of poverty which current
political humbug calls our prosperity and civilization.
Liberty is an excellent thing; but it cannot begin until
society has paid its daily debt to Nature by first earning its
living. There is no liberty before that except the liberty
to live at somebody else's expense, a liberty much sought
after nowadays, since it is the criterion of gentility, but not
wholesome from the point of view of the common weal.

SIEGFRIED CONCLUDED

In returning now to the adventures of Siegfried there is little
more to be described except the finale of an opera. Siegfried, having passed unharmed through the fire, wakes
Brynhild and goes through all the fancies and ecstasies of

love at first sight in a duet which ends with an apostrophe to "leuchtende Liebe, lachender Tod!", which has been romantically translated into "Love that illumines, laughing at death," whereas it really identifies enlightening love and laughing death as involving each other so closely as to be virtually one and the same thing.

NIGHT FALLS
ON THE GODS

Prologue

Die Götterdämmerung begins with an elaborate prologue. The three Norns sit in the night on Brynhild's mountain top spinning their thread of destiny, and telling the story of Wotan's sacrifice of his eye, and of his breaking off a bough from the world-ash to make a haft for his spear, also how the tree withered after suffering that violence. They have also some fresher news to discuss. Wotan, on the breaking of his spear by Siegfried, has called all his heroes to cut down the withered world-ash and stack its faggots in a mighty pyre about Valhalla. Then, with his broken spear in his hand, he has seated himself in state in the great hall, with the Gods and Heroes assembled about him as if in council, solemnly waiting for the end. All this belongs to the old legendary materials with which Wagner began *The Ring*.

The tale is broken by the thread snapping in the hands of the third Norn; for the hour has arrived when man has taken his destiny in his own hands to shape it for himself, and no longer bows to circumstance, environment, necessity (which he now freely wills), and all the rest of the inevitables. So the Norns recognize that the world has no further use for them, and sink into the earth to return to the First Mother.

Then the day dawns; and Siegfried and Brynhild come, and have another duet. He gives her his ring; and she gives him her horse. Away then he goes in search of more adventures; and she watches him from her crag until he disappears. The curtain falls; but we can still hear the trolling of his horn, and the merry clatter of his horse's shoes trotting gaily down the valley. The sound is lost in the grander rhythm of the Rhine as he reaches its banks. We hear again an echo of the lament of the Rhine maidens for the ravished gold; and then, finally, a new strain, which does not surge like the mighty flood of the river, but has an unmistakable tramp of hardy men and a strong land flavor about it. And on this the opera curtain at last goes up—for please remember that all that has gone before is only the overture.

The First Act

We now understand the new tramping strain. We are in the Rhineside hall of the Gibichungs, in the presence of King Gunther, his sister Gutrune, and Gunther's grim half brother Hagen, the villain of the piece. Gunther is a fool, and has for Hagen's intelligence the respect a fool always has for the brains of a scoundrel. Feebly fishing for compliments, he appeals to Hagen to pronounce him a fine fellow and a glory to the race of Gibich. Hagen declares that it is impossible to contemplate him without envy, but thinks it a pity that he has not yet found a wife glorious enough for him. Gunther doubts whether so extraordinary a person can possibly exist. Hagen then tells him of Brynhild and her rampart of fire; also of Siegfried. Gunther takes this rather in bad part, since not only is he afraid of the fire, but Siegfried, according to Hagen, is not, and will therefore achieve this desirable match himself. But Hagen points out that since Siegfried is riding about in quest of adventures, he will certainly pay an early visit to the renowned chief of the Gibichungs. They can then give him a philtre which will make him fall in love with Gutrune and forget every other woman he has yet seen.

Gunther is transported with admiration of Hagen's cunning when he takes in this plan; and he has hardly assented to it when Siegfried, with operatic opportuneness, drops in just as Hagen expected, and is duly drugged into the heartiest love for Gutrune, and total oblivion of Brynhild and his own past. When Gunther declares his longing for the bride who lies inaccessible within a palisade of flame, Siegfried at once offers to undertake the adventure for him. Hagen then explains to both of them that Siegfried can, after braving the fire, appear to Brynhild in the semblance of Gunther through the magic of the wishing-cap (or Tarnhelm, as it is called throughout *The Ring*), the use of which Siegfried now learns for the first time. It is of course part of the bargain that Gunther shall give his sister to Siegfried in marriage. On that they swear blood brotherhood; and at this opportunity the old operatic leaven breaks out amusingly in Wagner. With tremendous exordium of brass, the tenor and baritone go at it with a will, showing off the power of their voices, following each other in canonic imitation, singing together in thirds and sixths, and finishing with a lurid unison, quite in the manner of Ruy Gomez and Ernani, or Othello and Iago. Then without further ado Siegfried departs on his expedition, taking Gunther with him to the foot of the mountain, and leaving Hagen to guard the hall and sing a very fine solo which has often figured in the programs of the Richter concerts, explaining that his interest in the affair is that Siegfried will bring back the Ring, and that he, Hagen, will presently contrive to possess himself of that Ring and become Plutonic master of the world.

And now it will be asked how does Hagen know all about

the Plutonic empire; and why was he able to tell Gunther about Brynhild and Siegfried, and to explain to Siegfried the trick of the Tarnhelm. The explanation is that though Hagen's mother was the mother of Gunther, his father was not the illustrious Gibich, but no less a person than our old friend Alberic, who, like Wotan, has begotten a son to do for him what he cannot do for himself.

In the above incidents, those gentle moralizers who find the serious philosophy of the music dramas too terrifying for them, may allegorize pleasingly on the philtre as the maddening chalice of passion which, once tasted, causes the respectable man to forget his lawfully wedded wife and plunge into adventures which eventually lead him headlong to destruction.

We now come upon a last relic of the tragedy of Wotan. Returning to Brynhild's mountain, we find her visited by her sister Valkyrie Valtrauta, who has witnessed Wotan's solemn preparations with terror. She repeats to Brynhild the account already given by the Norns. Clinging in anguish to Wotan's knees, she has heard him mutter that were the ring returned to the daughters of the deep Rhine, both gods and world would be redeemed from that stage curse of Alberic's in *The Rhine Gold*. On this she has rushed on her war-horse through the air to beg Brynhild to give the Rhine back its ring. But this is asking Woman to give up love for the sake of Church and State. She declares that she will see them both perish first; and Valtrauta returns to Valhalla in despair. Whilst Brynhild is watching the course of the black thundercloud that marks her sister's flight, the fires of Loki again flame high round the mountain; and the horn of Siegfried is heard as he makes his way through them. But the man who now appears wears the Tarnhelm: his voice is a strange voice: his figure is the unknown one of the king of the Gibichungs. He tears the ring from her finger, and, claiming her as his wife, drives her into the cave without pity for her agony of horror, and sets Nothung between them in token of his loyalty to the friend he is impersonating. No explanation of this highway robbery of the ring is offered. Clearly, this Siegfried is not the Siegfried of the previous drama.

The Second Act

In the second act we return to the hall of Gibich, where Hagen, in the last hours of that night, still sits, his spear in his hand, and his shield beside him. At his knees crouches a dwarfish spectre, his father Alberic, still full of his old grievances against Wotan, and urging his son in his dreams to win back the ring for him. This Hagen swears to do; and as the apparition of his father vanishes, the sun rises and Siegfried suddenly comes from the river bank tucking into his belt the Tarnhelm, which has transported him from the mountain like the enchanted carpet of the Arabian tales. He describes his adventures to Gutrune until Gunther's boat is seen approaching, when Hagen seizes a cowhorn and calls the tribesmen to welcome their chief and his bride. It is most exhilarating, this colloquy with the startled and hastily armed clan, ending with a thundering chorus, the drums marking the time with mighty pulses from dominant to tonic, much as Rossini would have made them do if he had been a pupil of Beethoven's.

A terrible scene follows. Gunther leads his captive bride straight into the presence of Siegfried, whom she claims as her husband by the ring, which she is astonished to see on his finger: Gunther, as she supposes, having torn it from her the night before. Turning on Gunther, she says, "Since you took that ring from me, and married me with it, tell him of your right to it; and make him give it back to you." Gunther stammers, "The ring! I gave him no ring— er—do you know him?" The rejoinder is obvious. "Then where are you hiding the ring that you had from me?" Gunther's confusion enlightens her; and she calls Siegfried trickster and thief to his face. In vain he declares that he got the ring from no woman, but from a dragon whom he slew; for he is manifestly puzzled; and she, seizing her opportunity, accuses him before the clan of having played Gunther false with her.

Hereupon we have another grandiose operatic oath, Siegfried attesting his innocence on Hagen's spear, and Brynhild rushing to the footlights and thrusting him aside to attest his guilt, whilst the clansmen call upon their gods to send down lightnings and silence the perjured. The gods do not respond; and Siegfried, after whispering to Gunther that the Tarnhelm seems to have been only half effectual after all, laughs his way out of the general embarrassment and goes off merrily to prepare for his wedding, with his arm round Gutrune's waist, followed by the clan. Gunther, Hagen and Brynhild are left together to plot operatic vengeance. Brynhild, it appears, has enchanted Siegfried in such a fashion that no weapon can hurt him. She has, however, omitted to protect his back, since it is impossible that he should ever turn that to a foe. They agree accordingly that on the morrow a great hunt shall take place, at which Hagen shall thrust his spear into the hero's vulnerable back. The blame is to be laid on the tusk of a wild boar. Gunther, being a fool, is remorseful about his oath of blood brotherhood and about his sister's bereavement, without having the strength of mind to prevent the murder. The three burst into a herculean trio, similar in conception to that of the three conspirators in *Un Ballo in Maschera*; and the act concludes with a joyous strain heralding the appearance of Siegfried's wedding procession, with strewing of flowers, sacrificing to the gods, and carrying bride and bridegroom in triumph.

It will be seen that in this act we have lost all connection

with the earlier drama. Brynhild is not only not the Brynhild of *The Valkyrie*, she is the Hiordis of Ibsen, a majestically
savage woman, in whom jealousy and revenge are intensified
to heroic proportions. That is the inevitable theatrical
treatment of the murderous heroine of the Saga. Ibsen's
aim in *The Vikings* was purely theatrical, and not, as in his
later dramas, also philosophically symbolic. Wagner's aim
in *Siegfried's Death* was equally theatrical, and not, as it
afterwards became in the dramas of which Siegfried's
antagonist Wotan is the hero, likewise philosophically
symbolic. The two master dramatists therefore produce
practically the same version of Brynhild. Thus on the
second evening of *The Ring* we see Brynhild in the character
of the truth-divining instinct in religion, cast into an enchanted slumber and surrounded by the fires of hell lest she
should overthrow a Church corrupted by its alliance with
government. On the fourth evening, we find her swearing
a malicious lie to gratify her personal jealousy, and then
plotting a treacherous murder with a fool and a scoundrel.
In the original draft of *Siegfried's Death*, the incongruity is
carried still further by the conclusion, at which the dead
Brynhild, restored to her Godhead by Wotan, and again a
Valkyrie, carries the slain Siegfried to Valhalla to live there
happily ever after with its pious heroes.

As to Siegfried himself, he talks of women, both in this
second act and the next, with the air of a man of the world.
"Their tantrums," he says, "are soon over." Such speeches
do not belong to the novice of the preceding drama, but to
the original *Siegfried's Tod*, with its leading characters
sketched on the ordinary romantic lines from the old Sagas,
and not yet reminted as the original creations of Wagner's
genius whose acquaintance we have made on the two previous evenings. The very title "Siegfried's Death" survives
as a strong theatrical point in the following passage. Gunther, in his rage and despair, cries, "Save me, Hagen: save

my honor and thy mother's who bore us both." "Nothing
can save thee," replies Hagen: "neither brain nor hand, but
Siegfried's Death." And Gunther echoes with a shudder,
"*Siegfried's Death!*"

A WAGNERIAN NEWSPAPER CONTROVERSY

The devotion which Wagner's work inspires has been
illustrated lately in a public correspondence on this very
point. A writer in *The Daily Telegraph* having commented
on the falsehood uttered by Brynhild in accusing Siegfried
of having betrayed Gunther with her, a correspondence in
defence of the beloved heroine was opened in *The Daily
Chronicle.* The imputation of falsehood to Brynhild was
strongly resented and combated, in spite of the unanswerable
evidence of the text. It was contended that Brynhild's
statement must be taken as establishing the fact that she
actually was ravished by somebody whom she believed to be
Siegfried, and that since this somebody cannot have been
Siegfried, he being as incapable of treachery to Gunther as
she of falsehood, it must have been Gunther himself after a
second exchange of personalities not mentioned in the text.
The reply to this—if so obviously desperate a hypothesis
needs a reply—is that the text is perfectly explicit as to
Siegfried, disguised as Gunther, passing the night with
Brynhild with Nothung dividing them, and in the morning
bringing her down the mountain *through the fire* (an impassable
obstacle to Gunther) and there transporting himself in
a single breath, by the Tarnhelm's magic, back to the hall
of the Gibichungs, leaving the real Gunther to bring Brynhild down the river after him. One controversialist
actually pleaded for the expedition occupying two nights,
on the second of which the alleged outrage might have
taken place. But the time is accounted for to the last

minute: it all takes place during the single night watch of Hagen. There is no possible way out of the plain fact that Brynhild's accusation is to her own knowledge false; and the impossible ways just cited are only interesting as examples of the fanatical worship which Wagner and his creations have been able to inspire in minds of exceptional power and culture.

More plausible was the line taken by those who admitted the falsehood. Their contention was that when Wotan deprived Brynhild of her Godhead, he also deprived her of her former high moral attributes; so that Siegfried's kiss awakened an ordinary mortal jealous woman. But a goddess can become mortal and jealous without plunging at once into perjury and murder. Besides, this explanation involves the sacrifice of the whole significance of the allegory, and the reduction of *The Ring* to the plane of a child's conception of *The Sleeping Beauty*. Whoever does not understand that, in terms of the *Ring* philosophy, a change from Godhead to humanity is a step higher and not a degradation, misses the whole point of *The Ring*. It is precisely because the truthfulness of Brynhild is proof against Wotan's spells that he has to contrive the fire palisade with Loki, to protect the fictions and conventions of Valhalla against her.

The only tolerable view is the one supported by the known history of *The Ring*, and also, for musicians of sufficiently fine judgment, by the evidence of the scores; of which more anon. As a matter of fact Wagner began, as I have said, with *Siegfried's Death*. Then, wanting to develop the idea of Siegfried as neo-Protestant, he went on to *The Young Siegfried*. As a Protestant cannot be dramatically projected without a pontifical antagonist, *The Young Siegfried* led to *The Valkyrie*, and that again to its preface *The Rhine Gold* (the preface is always written after the book is finished). Finally, of course, the whole was revised. The revision, if carried out strictly, would have involved the cutting out of *Siegfried's Death*, now become inconsistent and superfluous; and that would have involved, in turn, the facing of the fact that *The Ring* was no longer a Niblung epic, and really demanded modern costumes, tall hats for Tarnhelms, factories for Nibelheims, villas for Valhallas, and so on—in short, a complete confession of the extent to which the old Niblung epic had become the merest pretext and name directory in the course of Wagner's travail. But, as Wagner's most eminent English interpreter once put it to me at Bayreuth between the acts of *Night Falls on the Gods*, the master wanted to "Lohengrinize" again after his long abstention from opera; and *Siegfried's Death* (first sketched in 1848, the year before the rising in Dresden and the subsequent events which so deepened Wagner's sense of life and the seriousness of art) gave him exactly the libretto he required for that outbreak of the old operatic Adam in him. So he changed it into *Die Götterdämmerung*, retaining the traditional plot of murder and jealousy, and with it, necessarily, his original second act, in spite of the incongruity of its Siegfried and Brynhild with the Siegfried and Brynhild of the allegory. As to the legendary matter about the world-ash and the destruction of Valhalla by Loki, it fitted in well enough; for though, allegorically, the blow by which Siegfried breaks the god's spear is the end of Wotan and of Valhalla, those who do not see the allegory, and take the story literally, like children, are sure to ask what becomes of Wotan after Siegfried gets past him up the mountain; and to this question the old tale told in *Night Falls on the Gods* is as good an answer as another. The very senselessness of the scenes of the Norns and of Valtrauta in relation to the three foregoing dramas, gives them a highly effective air of mystery; and no one ventures to challenge their consequentiality, because we are all more apt to pretend to understand great works of art than to confess that the meaning (if any) has escaped us. Valtrauta, however, betrays her irrelevance by explaining that the gods can be saved by the restoration of the ring to the Rhine daughters.

This, considered as part of the previous allegory, is nonsense; so that even this scene, which has a more plausible air of organic connection with *The Valkyrie* than any other in *Night Falls on the Gods*, is as clearly part of a different and earlier conception as the episode which concludes it, in which Siegfried actually robs Brynhild of her ring, though he has no recollection of having given it to her. *Night Falls on the Gods*, in fact, was not even revised into any real coherence with the world-poem which sprang from it; and that is the authentic solution of all the controversies which have arisen over it.

The Third Act

The hunting party comes off duly. Siegfried strays from it and meets the Rhine maidens, who almost succeed in coaxing the ring from him. He pretends to be afraid of his wife; and they chaff him as to her beating him and so forth; but when they add that the ring is accursed and will bring death upon him, he discloses to them as unconsciously as Julius Cæsar disclosed it long ago, that secret of heroism, never to let your life be shaped by fear of its end.[1] So he keeps the ring; and they leave him to his fate. The hunting party now finds him; and they all sit down together to make a meal by the river side, Siegfried telling them meanwhile the story of his adventures. When he approaches the subject of Brynhild, as to whom his memory is a blank, Hagen pours an antidote to the love philtre into his drinking horn, whereupon, his memory returning, he proceeds to narrate the incident of the fiery mountain, to Gunther's intense

---

[1] "We must learn to die, and to die in the fullest sense of the word. The fear of the end is the source of all lovelessness; and this fear is generated only when love begins to wane. How came it that this love, the highest blessedness to all things living, was so far lost sight of by the human race that at last it came to this: all that mankind did, ordered, and established, was conceived only in fear of the end! My poem sets this forth."—Wagner to Roeckel, 25th Jan. 1854.

mortification. Hagen then plunges his spear into the back of
Siegfried, who falls dead on his shield, but gets up again,
after the old operatic custom, to sing about thirty bars to his
love before allowing himself to be finally carried off to the
strains of the famous *Trauermarsch*.

The scene then changes to the hall of the Gibichungs by
the Rhine. It is night; and Gutrune, unable to sleep, and
haunted by all sorts of vague terrors, is waiting for the
return of her husband, and wondering whether a ghostly
figure she has seen gliding down to the river bank is Brynhild,
whose room is empty. Then comes the cry of Hagen,
returning with the hunting party to announce the death of
Siegfried by the tusk of a wild boar. But Gutrune divines
the truth; and Hagen does not deny it. Siegfried's body is
brought in; Gunther claims the ring; Hagen will not suffer
him to take it; they fight; and Gunther is slain. Hagen
then attempts to take it; but the dead man's hand closes on
it and raises itself threateningly. Then Brynhild comes; and
a funeral pyre is raised whilst she declaims a prolonged scena,
extremely moving and imposing, but yielding nothing to
resolute intellectual criticism except a very powerful and
elevated exploitation of theatrical pathos, psychologically
identical with the scene of Cleopatra and the dead Antony
in Shakespeare's tragedy. Finally she flings a torch into the
pyre, and rides her war-horse into the flames. The hall of
the Gibichungs catches fire, as most halls would were a
cremation attempted in the middle of the floor (I permit
myself this gibe purposely to emphasize the excessive
artificiality of the scene); but the Rhine overflows its banks to
allow the three Rhine maidens to take the ring from Siegfried's finger, incidentally extinguishing the conflagration as
it does so. Hagen attempts to snatch the ring from the
maidens, who promptly drown him; and in the distant
heavens the gods and their castle are seen perishing in the
fires of Loki as the curtain falls.

COLLAPSE OF THE ALLEGORY

In all this, it will be observed, there is nothing new. The musical fabric is enormously elaborate and gorgeous; but you cannot say, as you must in witnessing *The Rhine Gold*, *The Valkyrie*, and the first two acts of *Siegfried*, that you have never seen anything like it before, and that the inspiration is entirely original. Not only the action, but most of the poetry, might conceivably belong to an Elizabethan drama. The situation of Cleopatra and Antony is unconsciously reproduced without being bettered, or even equalled in point of majesty and musical expression. The loss of all simplicity and dignity, the impossibility of any credible scenic presentation of the incidents, and the extreme staginess of the conventions by which these impossibilities are got over, are no doubt covered from the popular eye by the overwhelming prestige of *Die Götterdämmerung* as part of so great a work as *The Ring*, and by the extraordinary storm of emotion and excitement which the music keeps up. But the very qualities that intoxicate the novice in music enlighten the adept. In spite of the fulness of the composer's technical accomplishment, the finished style and effortless mastery of harmony and instrumentation displayed, there is not a bar in the work which moves us as the same themes moved us in *The Valkyrie*, nor is anything but external splendor added to the life and humor of *Siegfried*.

In the original poem, Brynhild delays her self-immolation on the pyre of Siegfried to read the assembled choristers a homily on the efficacy of the Love panacea. "My holiest wisdom's hoard," she says, "now I make known to the world. I believe not in property, nor money, nor godliness, nor hearth and high place, nor pomp and peerage, nor contract and custom, but in Love. Let that only prevail; and ye shall be blest in weal or woe." Here the repudiations still smack of Bakoonin; but the saviour is no longer the volition of the full-grown spirit of Man, the Freewiller of Necessity, sword in hand, but simply Love, and not even Shelleyan Love, but vehement sexual passion. It is highly significant of the extent to which this uxorious commonplace lost its hold of Wagner (after disturbing his conscience, as he confesses to Roeckel, for years) that it disappears in the full score of *Night Falls on the Gods*, which was not completed until he was on the verge of producing *Parsifal*, twenty years after the publication of the poem. He cut the homily out, and composed the music of the final scene with a flagrant recklessness of the old intention. The rigorous logic with which representative musical themes are employed in the earlier dramas is here abandoned without scruple; and for the main theme at the conclusion he selects a rapturous passage sung by Sieglinda in the third act of *The Valkyrie* (p. 39, *ante*) when Brynhild inspires her with a sense of her high destiny as the mother of the unborn hero.   There is no dramatic logic whatever in the recurrence of this theme to express the transport in which Brynhild immolates herself. There is of course an excuse for it, inasmuch as both women have an impulse of self-sacrifice for the sake of Siegfried; but this is really hardly more than an excuse; since the Valhalla theme might be attached to Alberic on the no worse ground that both he and Wotan are inspired by ambition, and that the ambition has the same object, the possession of the ring.   The common sense of the matter is that the only themes which had fully retained their old hold on Wagner's intellectual conscience when he composed *Night Falls on the Gods* are those which are mere labels of external features, such as the Dragon, the Fire, the Water and so on.   This particular theme of Sieglinda's is, in truth, of no great musical merit: it might easily be the pet climax of a popular sentimental ballad: in fact, the gushing effect which is its sole valuable quality is so cheaply attained that it is hardly going too far to call it the most trumpery phrase in the entire tetralogy. Yet, since it undoubtedly does gush very emphatically, Wagner chose, for convenience' sake, to work up this final scene with it rather than with the more distinguished, elaborate and beautiful themes connected with the love of Brynhild and Siegfried.

He would certainly not have thought this a matter of no consequence had he finished the whole work ten years earlier. It must always be borne in mind that the poem of *The Ring* was complete and printed in 1853, and represents the sociological ideas which, after germinating in the European atmosphere for many years, had been brought home to Wagner, who was intensely susceptible to such ideas, by the crash of 1849 at Dresden. Now no man whose mind is alive and active, as Wagner's was to the day of his death, can keep his political and spiritual opinions, much less his philosophic consciousness, at a standstill for quarter of a century until he finishes an orchestral score. When Wagner first sketched *Night Falls on the Gods* he was thirty-five. When he finished the score for the first Bayreuth festival in 1876 he had turned sixty. No wonder he had lost his old grip of it and left it behind him. He even tampered with *The Rhine Gold* for the sake of theatrical effect when stage-managing it, making Wotan pick up and brandish a sword to give visible point to his sudden inspiration as to the raising up of a hero. The sword had first to be discovered by Fafnir among the Niblung treasures and thrown away by him as useless. There is no sense in this device; and its adoption shows the same recklessness as to the original intention which we find in the music of the last act of *The Dusk of the Gods*.[1]

---

[1] *Die Götterdämmerung* means literally *Godsgloaming*. The English versions of the opera are usually called *The Dusk of the Gods*, or *The Twilight of the Gods*. I have purposely introduced the ordinary title in the sentence above for the reader's information.

WHY HE CHANGED
HIS MIND

Wagner, however, was not the man to allow his grip of a great philosophic theme to slacken, even in twenty-five years, had the theme stood the test of the world's experience. If the history of Germany from 1849 to 1876 had been the history of Siegfried and Wotan transposed into the key of actual life, *Night Falls on the Gods* would have been the logical consummation of *The Rhine Gold* and *The Valkyrie* instead of the operatic anachronism it actually is.

But, as a matter of fact, Siegfried did not arrive and Bismarck did. Roeckel faded into a prisoner whose imprisonment made no difference. Bakoonin broke up, not Valhalla, but The International, which petered out in an undignified quarrel between him and Karl Marx. The Siegfrieds of 1848 were hopeless political failures, whereas the Wotans and Alberics and Lokis were conspicuous political successes. Even the Mimes held their own as against Siegfried. With the single exception of Ferdinand Lassalle, there was no revolutionary leader who was not an obvious Impossibilist in practical politics; and Lassalle got himself killed in a romantic and quite indefensible duel after wrecking his health in a titanic oratorical campaign which convinced him that the great majority of the working classes were not ready to join him, and that the minority who were ready did not understand him. The International, founded in 1864 by Karl Marx in London, and mistaken for several years by nervous newspapers for a red spectre, was really only a turnip ghost. It achieved some beginnings of international Trade Unionism by inducing English workmen to send money to support strikes on the continent, and recalling English workers who had been taken across the North Sea to defeat such strikes; but on its revolutionary socialistic side it was a romantic figment. The suppression of the Paris Commune, one of the most tragic examples in history of the pitilessness with which capable practical administrators and soldiers are forced by the pressure of facts to destroy romantic amateurs and theatrical dreamers, made an end of melodramatic Socialism. It was as easy for Marx, with his literary talent, to hold up Thiers as the most execrable of living scoundrels, and to put upon Gallifet a brand indelible enough to ostracize him politically for ever, as it was for Victor Hugo to bombard Napoleon III from his paper battery in Jersey. It was also easy to hold up Félix Pyat and Delescluze as men of much loftier ideals than Thiers and Gallifet; but the one fact that could not be denied was that when it came to actual shooting, it was Gallifet who got Delescluze shot and not Delescluze who got Gallifet shot, and that when it came to administering the affairs of France, Thiers could in one way or another get it done, whilst Pyat could neither do it nor stop talking and allow somebody else to do it. True, the penalty of following Thiers was to be exploited by the landlord and capitalist; but then the penalty of following Pyat was to be shot like a mad dog, or at best sent to New Caledonia, quite unnecessarily and uselessly.

To put it in terms of Wagner's allegory, Alberic had got the ring back again, and was marrying into the best Valhalla families with it. He had thought better of his old threat to dethrone Wotan and Loki. He had found that Nibelheim was a very gloomy place, and that if he wanted to live

handsomely and safely, he must not only allow Wotan and
Loki to organize society for him, but pay them very handsomely for doing it. He needed splendor, military glory,
loyalty, enthusiasm, and patriotism; and his greed and
gluttony were wholly unable to create them, whereas
Wotan and Loki carried them all to their most triumphant
climax in Germany in 1871, when Wagner himself celebrated
the event with his *Kaisermarsch*, which sounded much more
convincing than the *Marseillaise* or the *Carmagnole*.

How, after the *Kaisermarsch*, could Wagner go back to his
idealization of Siegfried in 1853? How could he believe
seriously in Siegfried slaying the dragon and charging
through the mountain fire, when the immediate foreground
was occupied by the Hôtel de Ville with Félix Pyat endlessly
discussing the principles of Socialism whilst the shells of
Thiers were already battering the Arc de Triomphe and
ripping up the pavement of the Champs Elysées? Is it not
clear that things had taken an altogether unexpected turn;
that although *The Ring* may, like the famous *Communist
Manifesto* of Marx and Engels, be an inspired guess at the
historic laws and predestined end of our capitalistic-theo-
cratic epoch, yet Wagner, like Marx, was too inexperienced
in technical government and administration and too melodramatic in his hero-contra-villain conception of the class
struggle, to foresee the actual process by which his generaliza-
tion would work out, or the part to be played in it by the
classes involved?

Let us go back for a moment to the point at which the
Niblung legend first becomes irreconcilable with Wagner's
allegory. Fafnir in the real world becomes a capitalist; but
Fafnir in the allegory is a mere hoarder. His gold does not
bring him in any revenue. It does not even support him;
he has to go out and forage for food and drink. In fact, he
is on the way to his drinking-pool when Siegfried kills him.
And Siegfried himself has no more use for the gold than

Fafnir: the only difference between them in this respect is that Siegfried does not waste his time watching a barren treasure that is useless to him, whereas Fafnir sacrifices his humanity and his life merely to prevent anybody else getting it. This contrast, true to human nature, is not true to modern economic development. The real Fafnir is not a miser: he seeks dividends, a comfortable life, and admission to the circles of Wotan and Loki. His only means of procuring these is to restore the gold to Alberic in exchange for scrip in Alberic's enterprises. Thus fortified with capital, Alberic exploits his fellow dwarfs as before, and also exploits Fafnir's fellow giants who have no capital. What is more, the competitive strategy and large-scaled enterprise the exploitation involves, and the self-respect and social esteem its success wins, effect a development in Alberic's own character which neither Marx nor Wagner appear to have foreseen. He discovers that to be a dull, greedy, narrow-minded money-grubber is not the way to make money on the modern scale; for though greed may suffice to turn tens into hundreds and even hundreds into thousands, to turn thousands into hundreds of thousands requires economic magnanimity and a will to power as well as to pelf. And to turn hundreds of thousands into millions, Alberic must make himself an earthly Providence for masses of workmen, creating towns, and governing markets. In the meantime, Fafnir, wallowing in the dividends he has done nothing to earn, may rot, intellectually and morally, from mere disuse of his energies and lack of incentive to excel; but the more impotent he becomes, the more dependent he is upon Alberic for his income, on Loki for his politics, and on Wotan for his respectability and safety from rebellion: Alberic, as the purse-bearer, being, under Destiny, the real master of the situation. Consequently, though Alberic in 1850 may have been merely the vulgar Manchester factory-owner portrayed in Friedrich Engels' *The Condition of the Working*

Class in England in 1844, in 1876 he was well on the way towards becoming exoterically a model philanthropic employer and esoterically a financier.

Now, without exaggerating the virtues of such gentlemen, it will be conceded by everybody except perhaps those veteran Social-Democrats who have made a cult of obsolescence under the name of Marxism, that the dominant sort of modern employer is not to be displaced and dismissed so lightly as Alberic in *The Ring*. Wotan is hardly less dependent on him than Fafnir: the War-Lord visits his works, acclaims them in stirring speeches, and imprisons his enemies; whilst Loki does his political jobs in Parliament, making wars and commercial treaties for him at command. And he owns and controls a new god, called The Press, which manufactures public opinion on his side, and organizes the persecution and suppression of Siegfried.

The end cannot come until Siegfried learns Alberic's trade and shoulders Alberic's burden. Not having as yet done so, he is still completely mastered by Alberic. He does not even rebel against him except when he is too stupid and ignorant, or too romantically impracticable, to see that Alberic's work, like Wotan's work and Loki's work, is necessary work, and that therefore Alberic can never be superseded by a warrior, but only by a capable man of business who is prepared to continue his work without a day's intermission. Even though the proletarians of all lands were to become "class-conscious," and obey the call of Marx by uniting to carry the class struggle to a proletarian victory in which all capital should become common property, and all Monarchs, Millionaires, Landlords and Capitalists become common citizens, the triumphant proletarians would have either to starve in anarchy next day or else do the political and industrial work which is now being done *tant bien que mal* by limited monarchs, despotic presidents, irresponsible financiers, and bourgeois parliaments. And in the meantime these magnates must defend their power and property with all their might against the revolutionary forces until these forces become positive, executive, administrative forces, instead of the conspiracies of protesting, moralizing, virtuously indignant amateurs who mistook Marx for a man of affairs and Thiers for a stage villain.

Now all this represents a development of which one gathers no forecast from Wagner or Marx. Both of them prophesied the end of our epoch; and, though in 1913 that epoch seemed so prosperous that the prophecy seemed ridiculously negligible, within ten years the centre had fallen out of Europe; and humane men could only shake their heads and shrug their shoulders when they were asked for another half-crown to help to save another ten million children from starvation. Alberic had prospered so greatly that he had come to believe himself immortal; and his alliances with Wotan had brought his sons and daughters under the influences, dangerous to commerce, of feudal militarist ideals. The abyss in his path had been pointed out to him not only by Wagner and Marx, but by men who, instead of vainly consulting the oracle in the pages of *Das Kapital*, had sought new and safe paths by the light of contemporary history and practical administrative experience. But Alberic would neither believe that the old path led to the abyss nor explore the new paths; and the masses knew nothing of paths and much of poverty. So he went faster and faster, at last marching sword in hand with his feudal sons-in-law, blasting his way with cyclopean explosives, at which point he crashed into the abyss he had not believed in, bringing down the civilization of Central and Eastern Europe along with him, and leaving the Bolshevists (*ci-devant* Marxists), Social-Democrats, Republicans and amorphous revolutionaries generally to extricate it as best they could, and to learn in the process the truth of these last few pages.

But Wagner did not live to see this reduction of Alberic to absurdity. What he did see was the reduction of Siegfried to absurdity. Siegfried had done nothing that promised success in his struggle with Alberic; and Alberic had not yet outdone Siegfried in ineptitude by committing suicide. Now Wagner was compelled by his profession to be, compared with Siegfried, a practical man. It is possible to learn more of the world by producing a single opera, or even conducting a single orchestral rehearsal, than by ten years reading in the library of the British Museum. Wagner must have learnt between *The Rhine Gold* and the *Kaisermarsch* that there are yet several dramas to be interpolated in *The Ring* after *The Valkyrie* before the allegory can tell the whole story. If anyone doubts the extent to which Wagner's eyes had been opened to the administrative childishness and romantic conceit of the heroes of the revolutionary generation that served its apprenticeship on the barricades of 1848–9, and perished on those of 1871 under Thiers' mitrailleuses, let him read *Eine Kapitulation*, that scandalous burlesque in which the poet and composer of *Siegfried*, with the levity of a schoolboy, mocked the French republicans who were doing in 1871 what he himself was exiled for doing in 1849. He had set the enthusiasm of the Dresden revolution to his own greatest music; but he set the enthusiasm of twenty years later in derision to the music of Rossini. There is no mistaking the tune he meant to suggest by his doggerel of Republik, Republik, Republik-lik-lik. The overture to *William Tell* is there as plainly as if it were noted down in full score.

In the case of such a man as Wagner, you cannot explain this *volte-face* as mere jingoism produced by Germany's overwhelming victory in the Franco-Prussian war, nor as personal spite against the Parisians for the *Tannhäuser* fiasco. Wagner had more cause for personal spite against his own countrymen than he ever had against the Parisians:

he was ten times bitterer against his respectable prosperity in Dresden than against his starvation in Paris. No doubt his outburst gratified the pettier feelings which great men have in common with small ones; but he was not a man to indulge in such gratifications or indeed to feel them as gratifications, if he had not become convinced of the administrative impotence of the agitators who were trying to wield Nothung, and who had done less for Wagner's own art than a single German king, and he, too, a mad one. Wagner had by that time done too much himself not to know that the world is ruled by deeds, not by good intentions, and that one efficient sinner is worth ten futile saints and martyrs.

I need not elaborate the point further in these pages. Like all men of genius, Wagner had exceptional sincerity, exceptional respect for facts, exceptional freedom from the hypnotic influence of sentimental popular movements, exceptional sense of the realities of political power as distinguished from the pretences and idolatries behind which the real masters of modern States pull their wires and train their guns. When he scored *Night Falls on the Gods*, he had accepted the failure of Siegfried and the triumph of the Wotan-Loki-Alberic trinity as a fact. He had given up dreaming of heroes, heroines, and final solutions, and had conceived a new protagonist in *Parsifal*, whom he announced, not as a hero, but as a fool, armed, not with a sword which cut irresistibly, but with a spear which he held only on condition that he did not use it: one who, instead of exulting in the slaughter of a dragon, was ashamed of having shot a swan. The change in the conception of the Deliverer could hardly be more complete. It reflects the change which took place in Wagner's mind between the composition of *The Rhine Gold* and *Night Falls on the Gods*; and it explains why he found it so easy to drop the *Ring* allegory and fall back on Lohengrinizing.

WAGNER'S OWN
EXPLANATION

And now, having given my explanation of *The Ring*, can I
give Wagner's explanation of it? If I could (and I can) I
should not by any means accept it as conclusive. Nearly
half a century has passed since the tetralogy was written; and
in that time the purposes of many half instinctive acts of
genius have become clearer to the common man than they
were to the doers. Some years ago, in the course of an
explanation of Ibsen's plays, I pointed out that it was by no
means certain or even likely that Ibsen was as definitely
conscious of his thesis as I. All the stupid people, and
some critics who, though not stupid, had not themselves
written what the Germans call "tendency" works, saw
nothing in this but a fantastic affectation of the extravagant
self-conceit of knowing more about Ibsen than Ibsen
himself. Fortunately, in taking exactly the same position
now with regard to Wagner, I can claim his own authority
to support me. "How," he wrote to Roeckel on the 23rd
August 1856, "can an artist expect that what he has felt
intuitively should be perfectly realized by others, seeing
that he himself feels in the presence of his work, if it is true
Art, that he is confronted by a riddle, about which he, too,
might have illusions, just as another might?"
   The truth is, we are apt to deify men of genius, exactly

as we deify the creative force of the universe, by attributing to logical design what is the result of blind instinct. What Wagner meant by "true Art" is the operation of the artist's instinct, which is just as blind as any other instinct. Mozart, asked for an explanation of his works, said frankly, "How do I know?" Wagner, being a philosopher and critic as well as a composer, was always looking for moral explanations of what he had created; and he hit on several very striking ones, all different. In the same way one can conceive Henry the Eighth speculating very brilliantly about the circulation of his own blood without getting as near the truth as Harvey did long after his death.

None the less, Wagner's own explanations are of exceptional interest. To begin with, there is a considerable portion of *The Ring*, especially the portraiture of our capitalistic industrial system from the socialist's point of view in the slavery of the Niblungs and the tyranny of Alberic, which is unmistakable, as it dramatizes that portion of human activity which lies well within the territory covered by our intellectual consciousness. All this is concrete Home Office business, so to speak: its meaning was as clear to Wagner as it is to us. Not so that part of the work which deals with the destiny of Wotan. And here, as it happened, Wagner's recollection of what he had been driving at was completely upset by his discovery, soon after the completion of *The Ring* poem, of Schopenhauer's famous treatise *The World as Will and Representation*. So obsessed did he become with this masterpiece of philosophic art that he declared that it contained the intellectual demonstration of the conflict of human forces which he himself had demonstrated artistically in his great poem. "I must confess," he writes to Roeckel, "to having arrived at a clear understanding of my own works of art through the help of another, who has provided me with the reasoned conceptions corresponding to my intuitive principles."

Schopenhauer, however, had done nothing of the sort. Wagner's determination to prove that he had been a Schopenhauerite all along without knowing it only shows how completely the fascination of the great treatise on *The Will* had run away with his memory. It is easy to see how this happened. Wagner says of himself that "seldom has there taken place in the soul of one and the same man so profound a division and estrangement between the intuitive or impulsive part of his nature and his consciously or reasonably formed ideas." And since Schopenhauer's great contribution to modern thought was to educate us into clear consciousness of this distinction—a distinction familiar, in a fanciful way, to the Ages of Faith and Art before the Renascence, but afterwards swamped in the Rationalism of that movement—it was inevitable that Wagner should jump at Schopenhauer's metaphysiology (I use a word less likely to be mistaken than metaphysics) as the very thing for him. But metaphysiology is one thing, political philosophy another. The political philosophy of Siegfried is exactly contrary to the political philosophy of Schopenhauer, although the same clear metaphysiological distinction between the instinctive part of man (his Will) and his reasoning faculty (dramatized in *The Ring* as Loki) is insisted on in both. The difference is that to Schopenhauer the Will is the universal tormentor of man, the author of that great evil, Life; whilst reason is the divine gift that is finally to overcome this life-creating will and lead, through its abnegation, to cessation and peace, annihilation and Nirvana. This is the doctrine of Pessimism. Now Wagner was, when he wrote *The Ring*, a most sanguine revolutionary Meliorist, contemptuous of the reasoning faculty, which he typified in the shifty, unreal, delusive Loki, and full of faith in the life-giving Will, which he typified in the glorious Siegfried. Not until he read Schopenhauer did he become bent on proving that he had always been a Pessimist at heart, and that Loki was the most sensible and worthy adviser of Wotan in *The Rhine Gold*.

Sometimes he faces the change in his opinions frankly enough. "My Niblung drama," he writes to Roeckel, "had taken form at a time when I had built up with my reason an optimistic world on Hellenic principles, believing that nothing was necessary for the realization of such a world but that men should wish it. I ingeniously set aside the problem why they did not wish it. I remember that it was with this definite creative purpose that I conceived the personality of Siegfried, with the intention of representing an existence free from pain." But he appeals to his earlier works to show that behind all these artificial optimistic ideas there was always with him an intuition of "the sublime tragedy of renunciation, the negation of the will." In trying to explain this, he is full of ideas philosophically, and full of the most amusing contradictions personally. Optimism, as an accidental excursion into the barren paths of reason on his own part, he calls "Hellenic." In others he denounces it as rank Judaism, the Jew having at that time become for him the whipping boy for all modern humanity. In a letter from London, he expounds Schopenhauer to Roeckel with enthusiasm, preaching the renunciation of the Will to Live as the redemption from all error and vain pursuits: in the next letter he resumes the subject with unabated interest, and finishes by mentioning that on leaving London he went to Geneva and underwent "a most beneficial course of hydropathy." Seven months before this he had written as follows: "Believe me, I too was once possessed by the idea of a country life. In order to become a radically healthy human being, I went two years ago to a Hydropathic Establishment, prepared to give up Art and everything if I could once more become a child of Nature. But, my good friend, I was obliged to laugh at my own naïveté when I found myself almost going mad. None of us will reach the promised land: we shall all die in the wilderness. Intellect is, as some one has said, a sort of disease: it is incurable."

Roeckel knew his man of old, and evidently pressed him for explanations of the inconsistencies of *The Ring* with *Night Falls on the Gods*. Wagner defended himself with unfailing cleverness and occasional petulances, ranging from such pleas as "I believe a true instinct has kept me from a too great definiteness; for it has been borne in on me that an absolute disclosure of the intention disturbs true insight," to a volley of explanations and commentaries on the explanations. He gets excited and annoyed because Roeckel will not admire the Brynhild of *Night Falls on the Gods*; reinvents the Tarnhelm scene; and finally, the case being desperate, exclaims, "It is wrong of you to challenge me to explain it in words: you must feel that something is being enacted that is not to be expressed in mere words."

THE PESSIMIST AS AMORIST

Sometimes he gets very far away from Pessimism indeed, and recommends Roeckel to solace his captivity, not by conquering the will to live at liberty, but by "the inspiring influences of the Beautiful." The next moment he throws over even Art for Life. "Where life ends," he says, very wittily, "Art begins. In youth we turn to Art, we know not why; and only when we have gone through with Art and come out on the other side, we learn to our cost that we have missed Life itself." His only comfort is that he is beloved. And on the subject of love he lets himself loose in a manner that would have roused the bitterest scorn in Schopenhauer, though, as we have seen (p. 65), it is highly characteristic of Wagner. "Love in its most perfect reality," he says, "is only possible between the sexes: it is only as man and woman that human beings can truly love. Every other manifestation of love can be traced back to that one absorbingly real feeling, of which all other affections are but an emanation, a connection, or an imitation. It is an error to look on this as only one of the forms in which love is revealed, as if there were other forms coequal with it, or even superior to it. He who after the manner of metaphysicians prefers *unreality* to *reality*, and derives the concrete from the abstract —in short, puts the word before the fact—may be right in esteeming the idea of love as higher than the expression of love, and may affirm that actual love made manifest in feeling is nothing but the outward and visible sign of a pre-existent, non-sensuous, abstract love; and he will do well to despise that sensuous function in general. In any case it were safe to bet that such a man had never loved or been loved as human beings can love, or he would have understood that in despising this feeling, what he condemned was its sensual expression, the outcome of man's animal nature, and not true human love. The highest satisfaction and expression of the individual is only to be found in his complete absorption, and that is only possible through love. Now a human being is both *man* and *woman*: it is only when these two are united that the real human being exists; and thus it is only by love that man and woman attain to the full measure of humanity. But when nowadays we talk of a human being, such heartless blockheads are we that quite involuntarily we only think of man. It is only in the union of man and woman by love (sensuous and supersensuous) that the human being exists; and as the human being cannot rise to the conception of anything higher than his own existence—his own being—so the transcendent act of his life is this consummation of his humanity through love."

It is clear after this utterance from the would-be Schopenhauerian, that Wagner's explanations of his works for the most part explain nothing but the mood in which he happened to be on the day he advanced them, or the train of thought suggested to his very susceptible imagination and active mind by the points raised by his questioner. Especially in his private letters, where his outpourings are modified by his dramatic consciousness of the personality of his correspondent, do we find him taking all manner of positions, and putting forward all sorts of cases which must be taken as clever and suggestive special pleadings, and not as serious and permanent expositions of his works. These works must speak for themselves: if *The Ring* says one thing, and a letter written afterwards says that it said something else, *The Ring* must be taken to confute the letter just as conclusively as if the two had been written by different hands. However, nobody fairly well acquainted with Wagner's utterances as a whole will find any unaccountable contradictions in them. As in all men of his type, our manifold nature was so marked in him that he was like several different men rolled into one. When he had exhausted himself in the character of the most pugnacious, aggressive, and sanguine of reformers, he rested himself as a Pessimist and Nirvanist. In *The Ring* the quietism of Brynhild's "Rest, rest, thou God" is sublime in its deep conviction; but you have only to turn back the pages to find the irrepressible bustle of Siegfried and the revelry of the clansmen expressed with equal zest. Wagner was not a Schopenhauerite every day in the week, nor even a Wagnerite. His mind changes as often as his mood. On Monday nothing will ever induce him to return to quill-driving: on Tuesday he begins a new pamphlet. On Wednesday he is impatient of the misapprehensions of people who cannot see how impossible it is for him to preside as a conductor over platform performances of fragments of his works, which can only be understood when presented strictly according to his intention on the stage: on Thursday he gets up a concert of Wagnerian selections, and when it is over writes to his friends describing how profoundly both bandsmen and audience were impressed. On Friday he exults in the self-assertion of Siegfried's will against all moral ordinances, and is full of a revolutionary sense of "the universal law of change and renewal": on Saturday he has an attack of holiness, and asks, "Can you conceive a moral action of which the root idea is not renunciation?" In short, Wagner can be quoted against himself almost without limit, much as Beethoven's adagios could be quoted against his scherzos if a dispute arose between two fools as to whether he was a melancholy man or a merry one.

THE MUSIC OF
THE RING

THE REPRESENTATIVE THEMES

To be able to follow the music of *The Ring*, all that is necessary is to become familiar enough with the brief musical phrases out of which it is built, to recognize them and attach a certain definite significance to them, exactly as any ordinary Englishman recognizes and attaches a definite significance to the opening bars of *God Save the Queen*. There is no difficulty here: every soldier is expected to learn and distinguish between different bugle calls and trumpet calls; and anyone who can do this can learn and distinguish between the representative themes or "leading motives" (Leitmotifs) of *The Ring*. They are the easier to learn because they are repeated again and again; and the main ones are so emphatically impressed on the ear whilst the spectator is looking for the first time at the objects, or witnessing the first strong dramatic expression of the ideas they denote, that the requisite association is formed unconsciously. The themes are neither long, nor complicated, nor difficult. Whoever can pick up the flourish of a coach-horn, the note of a bird, the rhythm of the postman's knock or of a horse's gallop, will be at no loss in picking up the themes of *The Ring*. No doubt, when it comes to forming the necessary

mental association with the theme, it may happen that the
spectator may find his ear conquering the tune more easily
than his mind conquers the thought.   But for the most part
the themes do not denote thoughts at all, but either emotions
of a quite simple universal kind, or the sights, sounds and
fancies common enough to be familiar to children.   Indeed
some of them are as frankly childish as any of the funny little
orchestral interludes which, in Haydn's *Creation*, introduce
the horse, the deer, or the worm.   We have both the horse
and the worm in *The Ring*, treated exactly in Haydn's manner, and with an effect not a whit less ridiculous to superior
people who decline to take it good-humoredly.   Even the
complaisance of good Wagnerites is occasionally rather
overstrained by the way in which Brynhild's allusions to her
charger Grani elicit from the band a little rum-ti-tum triplet
which by itself is in no way suggestive of a horse, although a
continuous rush of such triplets makes a very exciting
musical gallop.

Other themes denote objects which cannot be imitatively
suggested by music: for instance, music cannot suggest a
ring, and cannot suggest gold; yet each of these has a
representative theme which pervades the score in all
directions.   In the case of the gold, the association is
established by the very salient way in which the orchestra
breaks into the pretty theme in the first act of *The Rhine Gold*
at the moment when the sunrays strike down through the
water and light up the glittering treasure, hitherto invisible.
The reference of the strange little theme of the wishing-cap
is equally manifest from the first, since the spectator's
attention is wholly taken up with the Tarnhelm and its
magic when the theme is first pointedly uttered by the orchestra.   The sword theme is introduced at the end of *The
Rhine Gold* to express Wotan's hero inspiration; and I have
already mentioned that Wagner, unable, when it came to
practical stage management, to forego the appeal to the eye

as well as to the thought, here made Wotan pick up a sword and brandish it, though no such instruction appears in the printed score. When this sacrifice to Wagner's scepticism, as to the reality of any appeal to an audience that is not made through their bodily sense, is omitted, the association of the theme with the sword is not formed until that point in the first act of *The Valkyrie* at which Siegmund is left alone by Hunding's hearth, weaponless, with the assurance that he will have to fight for his life at dawn with his host. He recalls then how his father promised him a sword for his hour of need; and as he does so, a flicker from the dying fire is caught by the golden hilt of the sword in the tree, when the theme immediately begins to gleam through the quiver of sound from the orchestra, and only dies out as the fire sinks and the sword is once more hidden by the darkness. Later on, this theme, which is never silent whilst Sieglinda is dwelling on the story of the sword, leaps out into the most dazzling splendor the band can give it when Siegmund triumphantly draws the weapon from the tree. As it consists of seven notes only, with a very marked measure, and a melody like a simple flourish on a trumpet or post horn, nobody capable of catching a tune can easily miss it.

The Valhalla theme, sounded with solemn grandeur as the home of the gods first appears to us and to Wotan at the beginning of the second scene of *The Rhine Gold*, also cannot be mistaken. It, too, has a memorable rhythm; and its majestic harmonies, far from presenting those novel or curious problems in polyphony of which Wagner still stands suspected by superstitious people, are just those three simple chords which festive students who vamp accompaniments to comic songs "by ear" soon find sufficient for nearly all the popular tunes in the world.

On the other hand, the ring theme, when it begins to hurtle through the third scene of *The Rhine Gold*, cannot possibly be referred to any special feature in the general gloom and turmoil of the den of the dwarfs. It is not a melody, but merely the displaced metric accent which musicians call syncopation, rung on the notes of the familiar chord formed by piling three minor thirds on top of one another (technically, the chord of the minor ninth, *ci-devant* diminished seventh). One soon picks it up and identifies it; but it does not get introduced in the unequivocally clear fashion of the themes described above, or of that malignant monstrosity, the theme which denotes the curse on the gold. Consequently it cannot be said that the musical design of the work is perfectly clear at the first hearing as regards all the themes; but it is so as regards most of them, the main lines being laid down as emphatically and intelligibly as the dramatic motives in a Shakespearean play. As to the coyer subtleties of the score, their discovery provides fresh interest for repeated hearings, giving *The Ring* a Beethovenian inexhaustibility and toughness of wear.

The themes associated with the individual characters get stamped on the memory easily by the simple association of the sound of the theme with the appearance of the person indicated. Its appropriateness is generally pretty obvious. Thus, the entry of the giants is made to a vigorous stumping, tramping measure. Mimmy, being a quaint, weird old creature, has a quaint, weird theme of two thin chords that creep down eerily one to the other. Gutrune's theme is pretty and caressing: Gunther's, bold, rough, and commonplace. It is a favorite trick of Wagner's, when one of his characters is killed on the stage, to make the theme attached to that character weaken, fail, and fade away with a broken echo into silence.

THE CHARACTERIZATION

All this, however, is the mere child's play of theme work. The more complex characters, instead of having a simple

musical label attached to them, have their characteristic
ideas and aspirations identified with special representative
themes as they come into play in the drama; and the chief
merit of the thematic structure of *The Ring* is the mastery
with which the dramatic play of the ideas is reflected in the
contrapuntal play of the themes. We do not find Wotan,
like the dragon or the horse, or, for the matter of that, like
the stage demon in Weber's *Freischütz* or Meyerbeer's *Robert
the Devil*, with one fixed theme attached to him like a name
plate to an umbrella, blaring unaltered from the orchestra
whenever he steps on the stage. Sometimes we have the
Valhalla theme used to express the greatness of the gods as
an idea of Wotan's. Again, we have his spear, the symbol
of his power, identified with another theme, on which
Wagner finally exercises his favorite device by making it
break and fail, cut through, as it were, by the tearing sound
of the theme identified with the sword, when Siegfried
shivers the spear with the stroke of Nothung. Yet another
theme connected with Wotan is the Wanderer music which
breaks with such a majestic reassurance on the nightmare
terror of Mimmy when Wotan appears at the mouth of his
cave in the scene of the three riddles. Thus not only are
there several Wotan themes, but each varies in its inflexions
and shades of tone color according to its dramatic circumstances. So, too, the merry horn tune of the young Siegfried
changes its measure, loads itself with massive harmonies,
and becomes an exordium of the most imposing splendor
when it heralds his entry as full-fledged hero in the prologue
to *Night Falls on the Gods*. Even Mimmy has his two or three
themes: the weird one already described; the little one in
triple measure imitating the tap of his hammer, and fiercely
mocked in the savage laugh of Alberic at his death; and
finally the crooning tune in which he details all his motherly
kindnesses to the little foundling Siegfried. Besides this
there are all manner of little musical blinkings and

shamblings and whinings, the least hint of which from the orchestra at any moment instantly brings Mimmy to mind, whether he is on the stage at the time or not.

In truth, dramatic characterization in music cannot be carried very far by the use of representative themes. Mozart, the greatest of all masters of this art, never dreamt of employing them; and, extensively as they are used in *The Ring*, they do not enable Wagner to dispense with the Mozartian method. Apart from the themes, Siegfried and Mimmy are still as sharply distinguished from one another by the character of their music as Don Giovanni from Leporello, Wotan from Gutrune as Sarastro from Papagena. It is true that the themes attached to the characters have the same musical appropriateness as the rest of the music: for example, neither the Valhalla nor the spear themes could, without the most ludicrous incongruity, be used for the forest bird or the unstable, delusive Loki; but for all that the musical characterization must be regarded as independent of the specific themes, since the entire elimination of the thematic system from the score would leave the characters as well distinguished musically as they are at present.

One more illustration of the way in which the thematic system is worked. There are two themes connected with Loki. One is a rapid, sinuous, twisting, shifty semiquaver figure suggested by the unsubstantial, elusive logic-spinning of the clever one's braincraft. The other is the fire theme. In the first act of *Siegfried*, Mimmy makes his unavailing attempt to explain fear to Siegfried. With the horror fresh upon him of the sort of nightmare into which he has fallen after the departure of the Wanderer, and which has taken the form, at once fanciful and symbolic, of a delirious dread of light, he asks Siegfried whether he has never, whilst wandering in the forest, had his heart set hammering in frantic dread by the mysterious lights of the gloaming. To this, Siegfried, greatly astonished, replies that on such

occasions his heart is altogether healthy and his sensations
perfectly normal. Here Mimmy's question is accompanied
by the tremulous sounding of the fire theme with its harmonies most oppressively disturbed and troubled; whereas
with Siegfried's reply they become quite clear and straightforward, making the theme sound bold, brilliant, and
serene. This is a typical instance of the way in which the
themes are used.

The thematic system gives symphonic interest, reasonable-
ness, and unity to the music, enabling the composer to
exhaust every aspect and quality of his melodic material,
and, in Beethoven's manner, to work miracles of beauty,
expression and significance with the briefest phrases. As a
set-off against this, it has led Wagner to indulge in repetitions
that would be intolerable in a purely dramatic work.
Almost the first thing that a dramatist has to learn in con-
structing a play is that the persons must not come on the
stage in the second act and tell one another at great length
what the audience has already seen pass before its eyes in the
first act. The extent to which Wagner has been seduced
into violating this rule by his affection for his themes is
startling to a practised playwright. Siegfried inherits from
Wotan a mania for autobiography which leads him to inflict
on everyone he meets the story of Mimmy and the dragon,
although the audience have spent a whole evening witnessing
the events he is narrating. Hagen tells the story to Gunther;
and that same night Alberic's ghost tells it over again to
Hagen, who knows it already as well as the audience.
Siegfried tells the Rhine maidens as much of it as they will
listen to, and then keeps telling it to his hunting companions
until they kill him. Wotan's autobiography on the second
evening becomes his biography in the mouths of the Norns
on the fourth. The little that the Norns add to it is repeated
an hour later by Valtrauta. How far all this repetition is
tolerable is a matter of individual taste. A good story will

bear repetition; and if it has woven into it such pretty tunes as the Rhine maidens' yodel, Mimmy's tinkling anvil beat, the note of the forest bird, the call of Siegfried's horn, and so on, it will bear a good deal of rehearing. Those who have but newly learnt their way through *The Ring* will not readily admit that there is a bar too much repetition.

But how if you find some anti-Wagnerite raising the question whether the thematic system does not enable the composer to produce a music drama with much less musical fertility than was required from his predecessors for the composition of operas under the old system!

Such discussions are not within the scope of this little book. But as the book is now finished (for really nothing more need be said about *The Ring*), I am quite willing to add a few pages of ordinary musical criticism, partly to please the amateurs who enjoy that sort of reading, and partly for the guidance of those who wish to obtain some hints to help them through such critical small talk about Wagner and Bayreuth as may be forced upon them at the dinner table or between the acts.

THE OLD AND
THE NEW MUSIC

In the old-fashioned opera every separate number involved
the composition of a fresh melody; but it is quite a mistake
to suppose that this creative effort extended continuously
throughout the number from the first to the last bar. When
a musician composes according to a set metrical pattern, the
selection of the pattern and the composition of the first
stave (a stave in music corresponds to a line in verse)
generally completes the creative effort. All the rest follows
more or less mechanically to fill up the pattern, an air being
very like a wall-paper design in this respect. Thus the
second stave is usually a perfectly obvious consequence
of the first; and the third and fourth an exact or very slightly
varied repetition of the first and second. For example,
given the first line of *Pop Goes the Weasel* or *Yankee Doodle*, any
musical cobbler could supply the remaining three. There
is very little tune turning of this kind in *The Ring*; and it is
noteworthy that where it does occur, as in Siegmund's spring
song and Mimmy's croon, "Als zullendes Kind," the effect
of the symmetrical staves, recurring as a mere matter of
form, is perceptibly poor and platitudinous compared with
the free flow of melody which prevails elsewhere.

The other and harder way of composing is to take a
strain of free melody, and ring every variety of change of

mood upon it as if it were a thought that sometimes brought hope, sometimes melancholy, sometimes exultation, sometimes raging despair and so on.   To take several themes of this kind, and weave them together into a rich musical fabric passing panoramically before the ear with a continually varying flow of sentiment, is the highest feat of the musician: it is in this way that we get the fugue of Bach and the symphony of Beethoven.   The admittedly inferior musician is the only who, like Auber and Offenbach, not to mention our purveyors of drawingroom ballads, can produce an unlimited quantity of symmetrical tunes, but cannot weave themes symphonically.

When this is taken into account, it will be seen that the fact that there is a great deal of repetition in *The Ring* does not distinguish it from the old-fashioned operas.   The real difference is that in them the repetition was used for the mechanical completion of conventional metric patterns, whereas in *The Ring* the recurrence of the theme is an intelligent and interesting consequence of the recurrence of the dramatic phenomenon which it denotes.   It should be remembered also that the substitution of symphonically treated themes for tunes with symmetrical eight-bar staves and the like, has always been the rule in the highest forms of music.   To describe it, or be affected by it, as an abandonment of melody, is to confess oneself an ignoramus conversant only with dance tunes and ballads.

The sort of stuff a purely dramatic musician produces when he hampers himself with metric patterns in composition is not unlike what might have resulted in literature if Carlyle (for example) had been compelled by convention to write his historical stories in rhymed stanzas.   That is to say, it limits his fertility to an occasional phrase, and three quarters of the time exercises only his barren ingenuity in fitting rhymes and measures to it.   In literature the great masters of the art have long emancipated themselves from metric patterns. Nobody claims that the hierarchy of modern impassioned prose writers, from Bunyan to Ruskin, should be placed below the writers of pretty lyrics, from Herrick to Mr. Austin Dobson. Only in dramatic literature do we find the devastating tradition of blank verse still lingering, giving factitious prestige to the platitudes of dullards, and robbing the dramatic style of the genuine poet of its full natural endowment of variety, force and simplicity.

This state of things, as we have seen, finds its parallel in musical art, since music can be written in prose themes or in versified tunes; only here nobody dreams of disputing the greater difficulty of the prose forms, and the comparative triviality of versification. Yet in dramatic music, as in dramatic literature, the tradition of versification clings with the same pernicious results; and the opera, like the tragedy, is conventionally made like a wall paper. The theatre seems doomed to be in all things the last refuge of the hankering after cheap prettiness in art.

Unfortunately this confusion of the decorative with the dramatic element in both literature and music is maintained by the example of great masters in both arts. Very touching dramatic expression can be combined with decorative symmetry of versification when the artist happens to possess both the decorative and dramatic gifts, and to have cultivated both hand in hand. Shakespeare and Shelley, for instance, far from being hampered by the conventional obligation to write their dramas in verse, found it much the easiest and cheapest way of producing them. But if Shakespeare had been compelled by custom to write entirely in prose, all his ordinary dialogue might have been as good as the first scene of *As You Like It*; and all his lofty passages as fine as "What a piece of work is Man!", thus sparing us a great deal of blank verse in which the thought is common-place, and the expression, though catchingly turned, absurdly pompous. *The Cenci* might either have been a serious drama

or might never have been written at all if Shelley had not
been allowed to carry off its unreality by Elizabethan versification.   Still, both poets have achieved many passages in
which the decorative and dramatic qualities are not only
reconciled, but seem to enhance one another to a pitch
otherwise unattainable.

Just so in music.   When we find, as in the case of Mozart,
a prodigiously gifted and arduously trained musician who
is also, by a happy accident, a dramatist comparable to
Molière, the obligation to compose operas in versified
numbers not only does not embarrass him but actually
saves him trouble and thought.   No matter what his
dramatic mood may be, he expresses it in exquisite musical
verses more easily than a dramatist of ordinary singleness
of talent can express it in prose.   Accordingly, he too, like
Shakespeare and Shelley, leaves versified airs, like "Dalla
sua pace," or Gluck's "Che farò senza Euridice," or Weber's
"Leise, leise," which are as dramatic from the first note to
the last as the untrammelled themes of *The Ring*.   In
consequence, it used to be professorially demanded that all
dramatic music should present the same double aspect.
The demand was unreasonable, since symmetrical versification is no merit in dramatic music: one might as well
stipulate that a dinner fork should be constructed so as to
serve also as a tablecloth.   It was an ignorant demand too,
because it is not true that the composers of these exceptional
examples were always, or even often, able to combine
dramatic expression with symmetrical versification.   Side
by side with "Dalla sua pace" we have "Il mio tesoro" and
"Non mi dir," in which exquisitely expressive opening
phrases lead to decorative passages which are as grotesque
from the dramatic point of view as the music which Alberic
sings when he is slipping and sneezing in the Rhine mud is
from the decorative point of view.   Further, there is to be
considered the mass of shapeless "dry recitative" which

separates these symmetrical numbers, and which might have been raised to considerable dramatic and musical importance had it been incorporated into a continuous musical fabric by thematic treatment. Finally, Mozart's most dramatic finales and concerted numbers are more or less in sonata form, like symphonic movements, and must therefore be classed as musical prose. And sonata form dictates repetitions and recapitulations from which the perfectly unconventional form adopted by Wagner is free. On the whole, there is more scope for both repetition and convention in the old form than in the new; and the poorer a composer's musical gift is, the surer he is to resort to the eighteenth century patterns to eke out his invention.

THE NINETEENTH
CENTURY

When Wagner was born in 1813, music had newly become
the most astonishing, the most fascinating, the most miraculous art in the world. Mozart's *Don Giovanni* had made all
musical Europe conscious of the enchantments of the modern
orchestra and of the perfect adaptability of music to the
subtlest needs of the dramatist. Beethoven had shown how
those inarticulate mood-poems which surge through men
who have, like himself, no exceptional command of words,
can be written down in music as symphonies. Not that
Mozart and Beethoven invented these applications of their
art; but they were the first whose works made it clear that
the dramatic and subjective powers of sound were enthralling
enough to stand by themselves quite apart from the decorative musical structures of which they had hitherto been a
mere feature. After the finales in *Figaro* and *Don Giovanni*,
the possibility of the modern music drama lay bare. After
the symphonies of Beethoven it was certain that the poetry
that lies too deep for words does not lie too deep for music,
and that the vicissitudes of the soul, from the roughest fun to
the loftiest aspiration, can make symphonies without
the aid of dance tunes. As much, perhaps, will be claimed
for the preludes and fugues of Bach; but Bach's method was
unattainable: his compositions were wonderful webs of

exquisitely beautiful Gothic traceries in sound, quite beyond all ordinary human talent. Beethoven's far blunter craft was thoroughly popular and practicable: not to save his soul could he have drawn one long Gothic line in sound as Bach could, much less have woven several of them together with so apt a harmony that even when the composer is unmoved its progressions saturate themselves with the emotion which (as modern critics are a little apt to forget) springs as warmly from our delicately touched admiration as from our sympathies, and sometimes makes us give a composer credit for pathetic intentions which he does not entertain, just as a boy imagines a treasure of tenderness and noble wisdom in the beauty of a woman. Besides, Bach set comic dialogue to music exactly as he set the recitatives of the Passion, there being for him, apparently, only one recitative possible, and that the musically best. He reserved the expression of his merry mood for the regular set numbers in which he could make one of his wonderful contrapuntal traceries of pure ornament with the requisite gaiety of line and movement. Beethoven bowed to no ideal of beauty: he only sought the expression for his feeling. To him a joke was a joke; and if it sounded funny in music he was satisfied. Until the old habit of judging all music by its decorative symmetry had worn out, musicians were shocked by his symphonies, and, misunderstanding his integrity, openly questioned his sanity. But to those who were not looking for pretty new sound patterns, but were longing for the expression of their moods in music, he achieved a revelation, because, being single in his aim to express his own moods, he anticipated with revolutionary courage and frankness all the moods of the rising generations of the nineteenth century.

The result was inevitable. In the nineteenth century it was no longer necessary to be a born pattern designer in sound to be a composer. One had but to be a dramatist or a poet completely susceptible to the dramatic and descriptive powers of sound.   A race of literary and theatrical musicians appeared; and Meyerbeer, the first of them, made an extraordinary impression.   The frankly delirious description of his *Robert the Devil* in Balzac's short story entitled *Gambara*, and Goethe's astonishingly mistaken notion that he could have composed music for *Faust*, show how completely the enchantments of the new dramatic music upset the judgment of artists of eminent discernment.   Meyerbeer was, people said (old gentlemen still say so in Paris), the successor of Beethoven: he was, if a less perfect musician than Mozart, a profounder genius.   Above all, he was original and daring. Wagner himself raved about the duet in the fourth act of *Les Huguenots* as wildly as anyone.

Yet all this effect of originality and profundity was produced by a quite limited talent for turning striking phrases, exploiting certain curious and rather catching rhythms and modulations, and devising suggestive or eccentric instrumentation.   On its decorative side, it was the same phenomenon in music as the Baroque school in architecture: an energetic struggle to enliven organic decay by mechanical oddities and novelties.   Meyerbeer was no symphonist.   He could not apply the thematic system to his striking phrases, and so had to cobble them into metric patterns in the old style; and as he was no "absolute musician" either, he hardly got his metric patterns beyond mere quadrille tunes, which were either wholly undistinguished, or else made remarkable by certain brusqueries which, in the true rococo manner, owed their singularity to their senselessness.   He could produce neither a thorough music drama nor a charming opera.   But with all this, and worse, Meyerbeer had some genuine dramatic energy, and even passion; and sometimes rose to the occasion in a manner which, whilst the imagination of his contemporaries remained on fire with the novelties of dramatic music, led them to over-rate him with an extravagance which provoked

Wagner to conduct a long critical campaign against his supremacy. In the eighteen-sixties this was inevitably ascribed to the professional jealousy of a disappointed rival. Nowadays young people cannot understand how anyone could ever have taken Meyerbeer's influence seriously. The few who remember the reputation he built on *The Huguenots* and *The Prophet*, and who now realize what a no-thoroughfare the path he opened proved to be, even to himself, know how inevitable and how impersonal Wagner's attack was.

Wagner was the literary musician par excellence. He could not, like Mozart and Beethoven, produce decorative tone structures independently of any dramatic or poetic subject matter, because, that craft being no longer necessary for his purpose, he did not cultivate it. As Shakespeare, compared with Tennyson, appears to have an exclusively dramatic talent, so exactly does Wagner compared with Mendelssohn. On the other hand, he had not to go to third rate literary hacks for "librettos" to set to music: he produced his own dramatic poems, thus giving dramatic integrity to opera, and making symphony articulate. A Beethoven symphony (except the articulate part of the ninth) expresses noble feeling, but not thought: it has moods, but no ideas. Wagner added thought and produced the music drama. Mozart's loftiest opera, his *Ring*, so to speak, *The Magic Flute*, has a libretto which, though none the worse for seeming, like *The Rhine Gold*, the merest Christmas tomfoolery to shallow spectators, is the product of a talent immeasurably inferior to Mozart's own. The libretto of *Don Giovanni* is coarse and trivial: its transfiguration by Mozart's music may be a marvel; but nobody will venture to contend that such transfigurations, however seductive, can be as satisfactory as tone poetry or drama in which the musician and the poet are at the same level. Here, then, we have the simple secret of Wagner's pre-eminence as a dramatic musician. He wrote the poems as well as composed the music of his "stage festival plays," as he called them.

Up to a certain point in his career, Wagner paid the penalty of undertaking two arts instead of one. Mozart had his trade as a musician at his fingers' ends when he was twenty, because he had served an arduous apprenticeship to that trade and no other. Wagner was very far from having attained equal mastery at thirty-five: indeed he himself has told us that not until he had passed the age at which Mozart died did he compose with that complete spontaneity of musical expression which can only be attained by winning entire freedom from all preoccupation with the difficulties of technical processes. But when that time came, he was not only a consummate musician, like Mozart, but a dramatic poet and a critical and philosophical essayist, exercising a considerable influence on his century. The sign of this consummation was his ability at last to play with his art, and thus to add to his already famous achievements in sentimental drama that lighthearted art of comedy of which the greatest masters, like Molière and Mozart, are so much rarer than the tragedians and sentimentalists. It was then that he composed the first two acts of *Siegfried*, and later on *The Mastersingers*, a professedly comedic work, and a quite Mozartian garden of melody, hardly credible as the work of the straining artificer of *Tannhäuser*. Only, as no man ever learns to do one thing by doing something else, however closely allied the two things may be, Wagner still produced no music independently of his poems. The overture to *The Mastersingers* is delightful when you know what it is all about; but only those to whom it came as a concert piece without any such clue, and who judged its reckless counterpoint by the standard of Bach and of Mozart's *Magic Flute* overture, can realize how atrocious it used to sound to musicians of the old school. When I first heard it, with the clear march of the polyphony in Bach's *B minor Mass* fresh in my memory, I confess I thought that the parts had got dislocated, and that some parts of the band were half a bar behind the others.   Perhaps they were; but now that I am familiar with the work, and with Wagner's harmony, I can still quite understand certain passages producing that effect on an admirer of Bach even when performed with perfect accuracy.

THE MUSIC OF
THE FUTURE

The ultimate success of Wagner was so prodigious that to his
dazzled disciples it seemed that the age of what he called
"absolute" music must be at an end, and the musical future
destined to be an exclusively Wagnerian one inaugurated
at Bayreuth. All great geniuses produce this illusion.
Wagner did not begin a movement: he consummated it.
He was the summit of the nineteenth century school of
dramatic music in the same sense as Mozart was the summit
(the word is Gounod's) of the eighteenth century school.
All those who attempted to carry on his Bayreuth tradition
have shared the fate of the forgotten purveyors of second
hand Mozart a hundred years ago. As to the expected
supersession of absolute music, Wagner's successors in
European rank were Brahms, Elgar, and Richard Strauss.
The reputation of Brahms rests on his absolute music alone:
such works as his *German Requiem* endear themselves to us as
being musically great fun; but to take them quite seriously
is to make them oppressively dull. Elgar followed Beethoven
and Schumann: he owes nothing essential to Wagner, and
secured his niche in the temple by his symphonies and his
Enigma Variations, which are as absolutely musical as any
modern music can be. Although Strauss produced works
for the musical theatre which maintained it at the level

to which Wagner had raised it, his new departure was a form
of musical drama, comic epic, and soul autobiography in
which stage, singers, and all the rest of the theatrical
material of Bayreuth save only the orchestra are thrown
overboard, and the work effected by instrumental music
alone, even Beethoven's final innovation of a chorus being
discarded. Just the same thing happened when Elgar took
as his theme Shakespeare's *Henry IV*, with Falstaff as its
chief figure. He made the band do it all, and with such
masterful success that one cannot bear to think of what
would have been the result of a mere attempt to turn the
play into an opera.

The Russian composers whose vogue succeeded that of
Wagner were not in the least Wagnerian: they developed
from the romantic school, from Weber and Meyerbeer,
from Berlioz and Liszt, much as they might have done had
Wagner never existed except as a propagandist of the importance of their art. A disparaging attitude towards Wagner
resembling that of Chopin to Beethoven, and a very similar
escape from his influence even in technique, was quite
common among the composers whose early lives overlapped
the last part of his. In England the composers who are the
juniors of Elgar, but the seniors of (for example) Bax and
Ireland, the most notable of whom are Mr. Granville Bantock
and Mr. Rutland Boughton, were heavily Wagnerized in
their youth, and began by Tristanizing and Götterdäm-
merunging heroically; but when they found themselves
their Wagnerism vanished. The younger men do not begin
with Wagner nor even with Strauss: they are mostly bent on
producing curiosities of absolute music until they settle
down into a serious style of their own. All that can be said
for the Wagner tradition is that it finally killed the confusion
between decorative pattern music and dramatic music
which muddled Meyerbeer and imposed absurd repetitions
on the heroes and heroines of Handel and Mozart. Even in

absolute music, the post-Wagnerite sonata form has become so much less mechanical and thoughtless that the fact that it still persists in essentials is hardly worth asserting.

Writing before any of these developments had happened, I said in the first edition of this book that there was no more hope in attempts to out-Wagner Wagner in music drama than there had been in the old attempts to make Handel the starting point of a great school of oratorio. How true this was is now so obvious that my younger readers may wonder why I thought it worth while to say it. But if veterans did not indulge in these day-before-yesterdayisms Music would lose the thread of its history.

BAYREUTH

When the Bayreuth Festival Playhouse was at last completed, and opened in 1876 with the first performance of *The Ring*, European society was compelled to admit that Wagner was "a success." Royal personages, detesting his music, sat out the performances in the row of boxes set apart for princes. They all complimented him on the astonishing "push" with which, in the teeth of all obstacles, he had turned a fabulous and visionary project into a concrete commercial reality, patronized by the public at a pound a head. It is as well to know that these congratulations had no other effect upon Wagner than to open his eyes to the fact that the Bayreuth experiment, as an attempt to evade the ordinary social and commercial conditions of theatrical enterprise, was a failure. His own account of it contrasts the reality with his intentions in a vein which would be bitter if it were not so humorous. The precautions taken to keep the seats out of the hands of the frivolous public and in the hands of earnest disciples, banded together in little Wagner Societies throughout Europe, had ended in their forestalling by ticket speculators and their sale to just the sort of idle globe-trotting tourists against whom the temple was to have been strictly closed. The money, supposed to be contributed by the faithful, was begged by energetic subscription-hunting ladies from people who must have had the most grotesque misconceptions of the composer's aims: among others, the Khedive of Egypt and the Sultan of Turkey!

Since then, subscriptions are no longer needed; for the Festival Playhouse pays its own way now, and is commercially on the same footing as any other theatre. The only qualification required from the visitor is money. A Londoner spends twenty pounds on a visit: a native Bayreuther spends one pound. In either case "the Folk," on whose behalf Wagner turned out in 1849, are effectually excluded; and the Festival Playhouse must therefore be classed as infinitely less Wagnerian in its character than Hampton Court Palace. Nobody knew this better than Wagner; and nothing can be further off the mark than to chatter about Bayreuth as if it had succeeded in escaping from the conditions of our modern civilization any more than the Grand Opera in Paris or London.

Within these conditions, however, it effected a new departure in that excellent German institution, the summer theatre. Unlike the old opera houses, which are constructed so that the audience may present a splendid pageant to the delighted manager, it was designed to secure an uninterrupted view of the stage, and an undisturbed hearing of the music, to the audience. The dramatic purpose of the performances was taken with entire and elaborate seriousness as the sole purpose of them; and the management was jealous for the reputation of Wagner. The sightseeing globe-trotter no longer crowds out the genuine disciple: the audiences are now as genuinely devoted as Wagner could have desired: the disconcerted, bewildered, bored followers of fashion have vanished with the sportsman on a holiday: the atmosphere is the right one for the work. There is, apparently, an effective demand for summer theatres of the highest class. There is no reason why the experiment should not be tried in England. If our enthusiasm for Handel can support Handel Festivals, laughably dull, stupid and anti-Handelian as these choral monstrosities are, as well as annual provincial festivals on the same model, there is no likelihood of a Wagner

Festival failing.   Suppose, for instance, a Wagner theatre were built at Hampton Court or on Richmond Hill, not to say Margate pier, so that we could have a delightful summer evening holiday, Bayreuth fashion, passing the hours between the acts in the park or on the river before sunset, is it seriously contended that there would be any lack of visitors?   If a little of the money that is wasted on grand stands, Eiffel towers, and dismal Halls by the Sea, all as much tied to brief annual seasons as Bayreuth, were applied in this way, the profit would be far more certain and the social utility prodigiously greater.   Any English enthusiasm for Bayreuth that does not take the form of clamor for a Festival playhouse in England may be set aside as mere pilgrimage mania.

Besides, the early Bayreuth performances were far from delectable.   The singing was sometimes tolerable, and sometimes abominable.   Some of the singers were mere animated beer casks, too lazy and conceited to practise the self-control and physical training that is expected as a matter of course from an acrobat, a jockey or a pugilist. The women's dresses were prudish and absurd.   It is true that after some years Kundry no longer wore an early Victorian ball dress with "ruchings," and that Freia was provided with a quaintly modish copy of the flowered gown of spring in Botticelli's famous picture; but the mailclad Brynhild still climbed the mountains with her legs carefully hidden in a long white skirt, and looked so exactly like Mrs. Leo Hunter as Minerva that it was quite impossible to feel a ray of illusion whilst looking at her.   The ideal of womanly beauty aimed at, reminded Englishmen of the barmaids of the seventies, when the craze for golden hair was at its worst.   Further, whilst Wagner's stage directions were sometimes disregarded as unintelligently as at the old opera houses, Wagner's quaintly old-fashioned tradition of half rhetorical, half historical-pictorial attitude and gesture prevailed. The most striking moments of the drama were conceived as *tableaux vivants* with posed models, instead of as passages of action, motion and life.

I need hardly add that the supernatural powers of control attributed by credulous pilgrims to Wagner's widow, and later on to his son, did not exist. Prima donnas and tenors were as unmanageable at Bayreuth as anywhere else. Casts were capriciously changed; stage business was insufficiently rehearsed; the audience was compelled to listen to a Brynhild or Siegfried of fifty when they had carefully arranged to see one of twenty-five, much as in any ordinary opera house. Even the conductors upset the arrangements occasionally. On the other hand, we could always feel assured that in thoroughness of preparation of the chief work of the season, in strenuous artistic pretentiousness, in pious conviction that the work was of such enormous importance as to be worth doing well at all costs, the Bayreuth performances would deserve their reputation. Their example raised the quality of operatic performances throughout the world, even in apparently incorrigible centres of fashion and frivolity.

BAYREUTH IN ENGLAND

In 1898 I purposely dwelt on the early shortcomings of Bayreuth to shew that there was no reason in the world why as good and better performances of *The Ring* should not be given in England, and that neither Wagner's widow nor his son could pretend to handle them with greater authority than any artist who feels the impulse to interpret them. Nobody will ever know what Wagner himself thought of the artists who established the Bayreuth tradition: he was obviously not in a position to criticize them. For instance, had Rubini survived to create Siegmund, Wagner could hardly have written so amusing and vivid a description as he did of his Ottavio in the old Paris days. Wagner was under great obligations to the heroes and heroines of 1876; and he naturally said nothing to disparage their triumphs; but there is no reason to believe that all or indeed any of them satisfied him as Schnorr of Carolsfeld satisfied him as Tristan, or Schröder Devrient as Fidelio. It was just as likely that the next Schnorr or Schröder would arise in England. Nowadays it seems odd that anyone should need to be told all this. British and American singers have long since replaced the Bayreuth veterans to considerable advantage.

WAGNERIAN SINGERS

No nation need have any difficulty in producing a race of Wagnerian singers. With the single exception of Handel, no composer has written music so well calculated to make its singers vocal athletes as Wagner. Abominably as the Germans sang in Wagner's day, it was astonishing how they throve physically on his leading parts. His secret is the Handelian secret. Instead of specializing his vocal parts after the manner of Verdi and Gounod for shrieking sopranos, goat-bleating tenors, and tremulous baritones with an effective compass of about a fifth at the extreme tiptop of their ranges, and for contraltos with chest registers forced all over their compass in the manner of music hall singers, he employs the entire range of the human voice, demanding from everybody nearly two effective octaves. The bulk of the work lies easily in the middle of the voice, which is nevertheless well exercised all over, one part of it relieving the other healthily and continually. He uses the highest notes sparingly, and is ingeniously considerate in the matter of instrumental accompaniment. Even when the singer seems to dominate all the thunders of the full orchestra, a

glance at the score will shew that he is well heard, not because
of a stentorian voice, but because Wagner meant him to be
heard. The old lazy Italian style of orchestral accompaniment as we find it in Rossini's *Stabat* or Verdi's *Trovatore*,
where the strings play a rum-tum accompaniment whilst
the whole wind band blares away, fortissimo, in unison with
the singer, is somehow not so brutally opaque in practice as it
looks on paper; but Wagner never condescends to it. Even
in an ordinary opera house, with the orchestra ranged
directly between the singers and the audience, his instrumentation is transparent to the human voice.

On every point, then, a Wagner theatre and Wagner
festivals are much more generally practicable than the older
and more artificial forms of dramatic music. A presentable
performance of *The Ring* is a big undertaking only in the
sense in which the construction of a railway is a big undertaking: that is, it requires plenty of work and plenty of
professional skill; but it does not, like the old operas and
oratorios, require those extraordinary vocal gifts which only
a few individuals scattered here and there throughout
Europe are born with. Singers who could never execute
the roulades of Semiramis, Assur, and Arsaces in Rossini's
Semiramide, could sing the parts of Brynhild, Wotan, and
Erda without missing a note. Any Englishman can understand this if he considers for a moment the difference
between a Cathedral service and an Italian opera at Covent
Garden. The service is a much more serious matter than
the opera. Yet provincial talent is sufficient for it, if the
requisite industry and devotion are forthcoming. Even
at the Opera I have seen lusty troopers and porters, without
art or manners, accepted by fashion as principal tenors
during the long interval between Mario and Jean de Reszke;
and the two most extraordinary dramatic singers of the
twentieth century, Chaliapin and Vladimir Rosing, are
quite independent of the old metropolitan artificialities. Let

us remember that Bayreuth has recruited its Parsifals from the peasantry, and that the artisans of a village in the Bavarian Alps are capable of a famous and elaborate Passion Play, and then consider whether any country is so poor in talent that its amateurs must journey to the centre of Europe to witness a Wagner Festival.

WAGNERISM WITH WAGNER LEFT OUT

In spite of the fact that my old suggestion of a Festival Playhouse on Richmond Hill has now been proved perfectly feasible as far as the availability of the necessary home talent is concerned, only one serious attempt to establish a Bayreuth in England has come to my knowledge; and that one, far from concerning itself with Wagner, owes its success to native British music with some early ultra-classical assistance from Gluck. Mr. Rutland Boughton, who began his career as a composer when the influence of Wagner was at its height, has attempted to do in Somerset what Wagner did in Thuringia, with the very material difference that Wagner had the King of Bavaria at his back, and Mr. Boughton had nothing material at his back at all. He selected Glastonbury as his Bayreuth; and has established an annual festival there which can already shew a remarkable record of work done. The very desperation of the enterprise has been its salvation. Had Mr. Boughton been obsessed, as Wagner was, with the scale to which the Grand Operas of Paris, London, and Berlin work, he would have had to wait for a king to help him: that is, he would have waited for ever. Fortunately he remembered that Wagner was not only the highly professionalized royal conductor of Dresden, brought up in the belief that the only success that can hallmark an opera is a Meyerbeerian success at the Paris Opera: he was also the author of the saying that music is kept alive, not by the triumphs of fashionable commercial professionalism, but on the cottage piano of the amateur. Mr. Rutland Boughton began in ordinary village halls in Somerset, with a piano and his own fingers for orchestra, his wife as scene painter and costumier, and a fit-up for a stage. The singing and acting was done by the villagers and by anyone else who would come; and a surprising number of quite distinguished talents did come. On these terms performances were achieved which in point of atmosphere and intimacy of interest were actually better than the performances at the enormously more pretentious Festival Playhouse in Bayreuth, or its copy the Prince Regent Theatre in Munich. There were friendly subscribers, not enough to prevent each festival from ruining Mr. Boughton for six months or so, but enough to enable him to devote the remaining six months to preparation for another financial catastrophe, encouraged by the fact that the crashes were less and less disastrous as his enterprise became better and better known. His festival is now a yearly event in Avalon, once an island, now a city in a plain, Glastonbury, steeped in traditions which make it holy ground. But it still has no theatre, no electric light, no convenience for Wagnerian drama that every village does not possess. Yet it is here that the Wagnerist dream has been best realized in England.

That dream, truly interpreted, did not mean that the English soil should bring forth performances of Wagner's music copied from those at Bayreuth. It meant that the English soil should produce English music and English drama, and that English people should perform them in their own way. It is precisely because Mr. Boughton has never performed a work of Wagner's, but, with the scholastic exception of an opera or two by Gluck, has composed his own music, and had it and other English music sung in English ways, that he can claim to be a Perfect Wagnerite.

By this time there may be other and cognate experiments

less known to me. During the twentieth century an
important social development has transformed that costly
and deleterious bore, the British holiday, into a genuinely
recreative change. Under the title of Summer Schools,
voluntary associations of artistically minded students of
sociology, theosophy, science, history, and what not—shall
we say people who take life, or some department of life,
seriously, and cannot be happy unless they are using their
brains and learning something in the intervals of dancing
and singing for pure fun?—now appear every autumn in the
prettiest country districts. These Schools are open to
everybody; they afford intimate glimpses of more or less
celebrated people who come and lecture to them for the
sake of propaganda; and they are very much jollier, as well
as substantially cheaper and more genial, than the so-called
pleasure resorts in which irritable and overworked professional entertainers hypnotize credulous Britons into believing
that they are enjoying themselves when they are only paying
through the nose for being worried and pillaged. Where
there were formally only one or two elderly congresses, like
the meetings of the British Association, with no activity but
that of elderly lecturers all lecturing at the same time in
different rooms, there are now dozens of smaller but more
youthful and vital gatherings in which, whatever the main
subject to be studied may be, Art is continually breaking in
in one form or another.

I myself, after a larger experience of professionally and
commercially organized art than most men can afford (for
I had to earn my living as a critic of such art in my early
days), find that it is at such gatherings and from such
voluntary enterprises that I can oftenest recapture something
of that magic which music and drama had for me in my
childhood, and which it is so utterly impossible to preserve
under commercial conditions. Commerce in art can save
me from many ridiculous blunders and makeshifts that do

not matter; but it seldom achieves the things that do matter, never indeed except when they are forced on it in spite of its teeth by some individual artist, mostly one heavily persecuted by it as Wagner was.

Amateur art is discredited art in so far only as the amateur is known as the ape of commercial art. Persons who go to the theatre and opera house only to be smitten with an infatuate ambition to reproduce in their own untrained persons what they see the great professional artists doing there, are mostly foredoomed to failure and ridicule. Here and there one of them succeeds, only to be absorbed by the commercial profession. But the countryside is full of stout characters with no such folly and no such ambition, who will do as much for any really gifted artistic leader as they have done for Mr. Boughton and for the organizers of our provincial choirs and brass bands. If Little Bethel has raised the miners of England in a few generations from troglodyte savagery to pious respectability, Little Bayreuth may as easily raise them from pious respectability to a happy consciousness of and interest in fine art, without which all their piety and respectability will not save their children from resorting to cruel sports and squalid sensualities in their natural need for enjoyment. And so, good luck to Little Bayreuth; and may it be as successful as Little Bethel in demonstrating that the laughter of fools is as the crackling of thorns under a pot!

CATALOGUE OF DOVER BOOKS

Books Explaining Science and Mathematics

WHAT IS SCIENCE?, N. Campbell. The role of experiment and measurement, the function of mathematics, the nature of scientific laws, the difference between laws and theories, the limitations of science, and many similarly provocative topics are treated clearly and without technicalities by an eminent scientist. "Still an excellent introduction to scientific philosophy," H. Margenau in PHYSICS TODAY. "A first-rate primer . . . deserves a wide audience," SCIENTIFIC AMERICAN. 192pp. 5⅜ x 8.   S43 Paperbound **$1.25**

THE NATURE OF PHYSICAL THEORY, P. W. Bridgman. A Nobel Laureate's clear, non-technical lectures on difficulties and paradoxes connected with frontier research on the physical sciences. Concerned with such central concepts as thought, logic, mathematics, relativity, probability, wave mechanics, etc. he analyzes the contributions of such men as Newton, Einstein, Bohr, Heisenberg, and many others. "Lucid and entertaining . . . recommended to anyone who wants to get some insight into current philosophies of science," THE NEW PHILOSOPHY. Index. xi + 138pp. 5⅜ x 8.   S33 Paperbound **$1.25**

EXPERIMENT AND THEORY IN PHYSICS, Max Born. A Nobel Laureate examines the nature of experiment and theory in theoretical physics and analyzes the advances made by the great physicists of our day: Heisenberg, Einstein, Bohr, Planck, Dirac, and others. The actual process of creation is detailed step-by-step by one who participated. A fine examination of the scientific method at work. 44pp. 5⅜ x 8.   S308 Paperbound **75¢**

THE PSYCHOLOGY OF INVENTION IN THE MATHEMATICAL FIELD, J. Hadamard. The reports of such men as Descartes, Pascal, Einstein, Poincaré, and others are considered in this investigation of the method of idea-creation in mathematics and other sciences and the thinking process in general. How do ideas originate? What is the role of the unconscious? What is Poincaré's forgetting hypothesis? are some of the fascinating questions treated. A penetrating analysis of Einstein's thought processes concludes the book. xiii + 145pp. 5⅜ x 8.   T107 Paperbound **$1.25**

THE NATURE OF LIGHT AND COLOUR IN THE OPEN AIR, M. Minnaert. Why are shadows sometimes blue, sometimes green, or other colors depending on the light and surroundings? What causes mirages? Why do multiple suns and moons appear in the sky? Professor Minnaert explains these unusual phenomena and hundreds of others in simple, easy-to-understand terms based on optical laws and the properties of light and color. No mathematics is required but artists, scientists, students, and everyone fascinated by these "tricks" of nature will find thousands of useful and amazing pieces of information. Hundreds of observational experiments are suggested which require no special equipment. 200 illustrations; 42 photos. xvi + 362pp. 5⅜ x 8.   T196 Paperbound **$2.00**

THE UNIVERSE OF LIGHT, W. Bragg. Sir William Bragg, Nobel Laureate and great modern physicist, is also well known for his powers of clear exposition. Here he analyzes all aspects of light for the layman: lenses, reflection, refraction, the optics of vision, x-rays, the photoelectric effect, etc. He tells you what causes the color of spectra, rainbows, and soap bubbles, how magic mirrors work, and much more. Dozens of simple experiments are described. Preface. Index. 199 line drawings and photographs, including 2 full-page color plates. x + 283pp. 5⅜ x 8.   T538 Paperbound **$1.85**

SOAP-BUBBLES: THEIR COLOURS AND THE FORCES THAT MOULD THEM, C. V. Boys. For continuing popularity and validity as scientific primer, few books can match this volume of easily-followed experiments, explanations. Lucid exposition of complexities of liquid films, surface tension and related phenomena, bubbles' reaction to heat, motion, music, magnetic fields. Experiments with capillary attraction, soap bubbles on frames, composite bubbles, liquid cylinders and jets, bubbles other than soap, etc. Wonderful introduction to scientific method, natural laws that have many ramifications in areas of modern physics. Only complete edition in print. New Introduction by S. Z. Lewin, New York University. 83 illustrations; 1 full-page color plate. xii + 190pp. 5⅜ x 8½.   T542 Paperbound **95¢**

THE STORY OF X-RAYS FROM RONTGEN TO ISOTOPES, A. R. Bleich, M.D. This book, by a member of the American College of Radiology, gives the scientific explanation of x-rays, their applications in medicine, industry and art, and their danger (and that of atmospheric radiation) to the individual and the species. You learn how radiation therapy is applied against cancer, how x-rays diagnose heart disease and other ailments, how they are used to examine mummies for information on diseases of early societies, and industrial materials for hidden weaknesses. 54 illustrations show x-rays of flowers, bones, stomach, gears with flaws, etc. 1st publication. Index. xix + 186pp. 5⅜ x 8. T622 Paperbound **$1.50**

SPINNING TOPS AND GYROSCOPIC MOTION, John Perry. A classic elementary text of the dynamics of rotation — the behavior and use of rotating bodies such as gyroscopes and tops. In simple, everyday English you are shown how quasi-rigidity is induced in discs of paper, smoke rings, chains, etc., by rapid motions; why a gyrostat falls and why a top rises; precession; how the earth's motion affects climate; and many other phenomena. Appendix on practical use of gyroscopes. 62 figures. 128pp. 5⅜ x 8. T416 Paperbound **$1.25**

SNOW CRYSTALS, W. A. Bentley, M. J. Humphreys. For almost 50 years W. A. Bentley photographed snow flakes in his laboratory in Jericho, Vermont; in 1931 the American Meteorological Society gathered together the best of his work, some 2400 photographs of snow flakes, plus a few ice flowers, windowpane frosts, dew, frozen rain, and other ice formations. Pictures were selected for beauty and scientific value. A very valuable work to anyone in meteorology, cryology; most interesting to layman; extremely useful for artist who wants beautiful, crystalline designs. All copyright free. Unabridged reprint of 1931 edition. 2453 illustrations. 227pp. 8 x 10½. T287 Paperbound **$3.00**

A DOVER SCIENCE SAMPLER, edited by George Barkin. A collection of brief, non-technical passages from 44 Dover Books Explaining Science for the enjoyment of the science-minded browser. Includes work of Bertrand Russell, Poincaré, Laplace, Max Born, Galileo, Newton; material on physics, mathematics, metallurgy, anatomy, astronomy, chemistry, etc. You will be fascinated by Martin Gardner's analysis of the sincere pseudo-scientist, Moritz's account of Newton's absentmindedness, Bernard's examples of human vivisection, etc. Illustrations from the Diderot Pictorial Encyclopedia and De Re Metallica. 64 pages. **FREE**

THE STORY OF ATOMIC THEORY AND ATOMIC ENERGY, J. G. Feinberg. A broader approach to subject of nuclear energy and its cultural implications than any other similar source. Very readable, informal, completely non-technical text. Begins with first atomic theory, 600 B.C. and carries you through the work of Mendelejeff, Röntgen, Madame Curie, to Einstein's equation and the A-bomb. New chapter goes through thermonuclear fission, binding energy, other events up to 1959. Radioactive decay and radiation hazards, future benefits, work of Bohr, moderns, hundreds more topics. "Deserves special mention . . . not only authoritative but thoroughly popular in the best sense of the word," Saturday Review. Formerly, "The Atom Story." Expanded with new chapter. Three appendixes. Index. 34 illustrations. vii + 243pp. 5⅜ x 8. T625 Paperbound **$1.60**

THE STRANGE STORY OF THE QUANTUM, AN ACCOUNT FOR THE GENERAL READER OF THE GROWTH OF IDEAS UNDERLYING OUR PRESENT ATOMIC KNOWLEDGE, B. Hoffmann. Presents lucidly and expertly, with barest amount of mathematics, the problems and theories which led to modern quantum physics. Dr. Hoffmann begins with the closing years of the 19th century, when certain trifling discrepancies were noticed, and with illuminating analogies and examples takes you through the brilliant concepts of Planck, Einstein, Pauli, Broglie, Bohr, Schroedinger, Heisenberg, Dirac, Sommerfeld, Feynman, etc. This edition includes a new, long postscript carrying the story through 1958. "Of the books attempting an account of the history and contents of our modern atomic physics which have come to my attention, this is the best," H. Margenau, Yale University, in "American Journal of Physics." 32 tables and line illustrations. Index. 275pp. 5⅜ x 8. T518 Paperbound **$1.50**

SPACE AND TIME, E. Borel. Written by a versatile mathematician of world renown with his customary lucidity and precision, this introduction to relativity for the layman presents scores of examples, analogies, and illustrations that open up new ways of thinking about space and time. It covers abstract geometry and geographical maps, continuity and topology, the propagation of light, the special theory of relativity, the general theory of relativity, theoretical researches, and much more. Mathematical notes. 2 Indexes. 4 Appendices. 15 figures. xvi + 243pp. 5⅜ x 8. T592 Paperbound **$1.75**

FROM EUCLID TO EDDINGTON: A STUDY OF THE CONCEPTIONS OF THE EXTERNAL WORLD, Sir Edmund Whittaker. A foremost British scientist traces the development of theories of natural philosophy from the western rediscovery of Euclid to Eddington, Einstein, Dirac, etc. The inadequacy of classical physics is contrasted with present day attempts to understand the physical world through relativity, non-Euclidean geometry, space curvature, wave mechanics, etc. 5 major divisions of examination: Space; Time and Movement; the Concepts of Classical Physics; the Concepts of Quantum Mechanics; the Eddington Universe 212pp. 5⅜ x 8. T491 Paperbound **$1.35**

Nature, Biology,

NATURE RECREATION: Group Guidance for the Out-of-doors, William Gould Vinal. Intended for both the uninitiated nature instructor and the education student on the college level, this complete "how-to" program surveys the entire area of nature education for the young. Philosophy of nature recreation; requirements, responsibilities, important information for group leaders; nature games; suggested group projects; conducting meetings and getting discussions started; etc. Scores of immediately applicable teaching aids, plus completely updated sources of information, pamphlets, field guides, recordings, etc. Bibliography. 74 photographs. + 310pp. 5⅜ x 8½. T1015 Paperbound **$1.75**

HOW TO KNOW THE WILD FLOWERS, Mrs. William Starr Dana. Classic nature book that has introduced thousands to wonders of American wild flowers. Color-season principle of organization is easy to use, even by those with no botanical training, and the genial, refreshing discussions of history, folklore, uses of over 1,000 native and escape flowers, foliage plants are informative as well as fun to read. Over 170 full-page plates, collected from several editions, may be colored in to make permanent records of finds. Revised to conform with 1950 edition of Gray's Manual of Botany. xlii + 438pp. 5⅜ x 8½. T332 Paperbound **$2.00**

HOW TO KNOW THE FERNS, F. T. Parsons. Ferns, among our most lovely native plants, are all too little known. This classic of nature lore will enable the layman to identify almost any American fern he may come across. After an introduction on the structure and life of ferns, the 57 most important ferns are fully pictured and described (arranged upon a simple identification key). Index of Latin and English names. 61 illustrations and 42 full-page plates. xiv + 215pp. 5⅜ x 8. T740 Paperbound **$1.35**

MANUAL OF THE TREES OF NORTH AMERICA, Charles Sprague Sargent. Still unsurpassed as most comprehensive, reliable study of North American tree characteristics, precise locations and distribution. By dean of American dendrologists. Every tree native to U.S., Canada, Alaska, 185 genera, 717 species, described in detail—leaves, flowers, fruit, winterbuds, bark, wood, growth habits etc. plus discussion of varieties and local variants, immaturity variations. Over 100 keys, including unusual 11-page analytical key to genera, aid in identification. 783 clear illustrations of flowers, fruit, leaves. An unmatched permanent reference work for all nature lovers. Second enlarged (1926) edition. Synopsis of families. Analytical key to genera. Glossary of technical terms. Index. 783 illustrations, 1 map. Two volumes. Total of 982pp. 5⅜ x 8. T277 Vol. I Paperbound **$2.25**
T278 Vol. II Paperbound **$2.25**
The set **$4.50**

TREES OF THE EASTERN AND CENTRAL UNITED STATES AND CANADA, W. M. Harlow. A revised edition of a standard middle-level guide to native trees and important escapes. More than 140 trees are described in detail, and illustrated with more than 600 drawings and photographs. Supplementary keys will enable the careful reader to identify almost any tree he might encounter. xiii + 288pp. 5⅜ x 8. T395 Paperbound **$1.35**

GUIDE TO SOUTHERN TREES, Ellwood S. Harrar and J. George Harrar. All the essential information about trees indigenous to the South, in an extremely handy format. Introductory essay on methods of tree classification and study, nomenclature, chief divisions of Southern trees, etc. Approximately 100 keys and synopses allow for swift, accurate identification of trees. Numerous excellent illustrations, non-technical text make this a useful book for teachers of biology or natural science, nature lovers, amateur naturalists. Revised 1962 edition. Index. Bibliography. Glossary of technical terms. 920 illustrations; 201 full-page plates. ix + 709pp. 4⅝ x 6⅜. T945 Paperbound **$2.35**

FRUIT KEY AND TWIG KEY TO TREES AND SHRUBS, W. M. Harlow. Bound together in one volume for the first time, these handy and accurate keys to fruit and twig identification are the only guides of their sort with photographs (up to 3 times natural size). "Fruit Key": Key to over 120 different deciduous and evergreen fruits. 139 photographs and 11 line drawings. Synoptic summary of fruit types. Bibliography. 2 Indexes (common and scientific names). "Twig Key": Key to over 160 different twigs and buds. 173 photographs. Glossary of technical terms. Bibliography. 2 Indexes (common and scientific names). Two volumes bound as one. Total of xvii + 126pp. 5⅜ x 8⅜. T511 Paperbound **$1.25**

INSECT LIFE AND INSECT NATURAL HISTORY, S. W. Frost. A work emphasizing habits, social life, and ecological relations of insects, rather than more academic aspects of classification and morphology. Prof. Frost's enthusiasm and knowledge are everywhere evident as he discusses insect associations and specialized habits like leaf-rolling, leaf-mining, and case-making, the gall insects, the boring insects, aquatic insects, etc. He examines all sorts of matters not usually covered in general works, such as: insects as human food, insect music and musicians, insect response to electric and radio waves, use of insects in art and literature. The admirably executed purpose of this book, which covers the middle ground between elementary treatment and scholarly monographs, is to excite the reader to observe for himself. Over 700 illustrations. Extensive bibliography. x + 524pp. 5⅜ x 8. T517 Paperbound **$2.50**

COMMON SPIDERS OF THE UNITED STATES, J. H. Emerton. Here is a nature hobby you can pursue right in your own cellar! Only non-technical, but thorough, reliable guide to spiders for the layman. Over 200 spiders from all parts of the country, arranged by scientific classification, are identified by shape and color, number of eyes, habitat and range, habits, etc. Full text, 501 line drawings and photographs, and valuable introduction explain webs, poisons, threads, capturing and preserving spiders, etc. Index. New synoptic key by S. W. Frost. xxiv + 225pp. 5⅜ x 8. **T223 Paperbound $1.45**

THE LIFE STORY OF THE FISH: HIS MANNERS AND MORALS, Brian Curtis. A comprehensive, non-technical survey of just about everything worth knowing about fish. Written for the aquarist, the angler, and the layman with an inquisitive mind, the text covers such topics as evolution, external covering and protective coloration, physics and physiology of vision, maintenance of equilibrium, function of the lateral line canal for auditory and temperature senses, nervous system, function of the air bladder, reproductive system and methods—courtship, mating, spawning, care of young—and many more. Also sections on game fish, the problems of conservation and a fascinating chapter on fish curiosities. "Clear, simple language . . . excellent judgment in choice of subjects . . . delightful sense of humor," New York Times. Revised (1949) edition. Index. Bibliography of 72 items. 6 full-page photographic plates. xii + 284pp. 5⅜ x 8. **T929 Paperbound $1.65**

BATS, Glover Morrill Allen. The most comprehensive study of bats as a life-form by the world's foremost authority. A thorough summary of just about everything known about this fascinating and mysterious flying mammal, including its unique location sense, hibernation and cycles, its habitats and distribution, its wing structure and flying habits, and its relationship to man in the long history of folklore and superstition. Written on a middle-level, the book can be profitably studied by a trained zoologist and thoroughly enjoyed by the layman. "An absorbing text with excellent illustrations. Bats should have more friends and fewer thoughtless detractors as a result of the publication of this volume," William Beebe, Books. Extensive bibliography. 57 photographs and illustrations. x + 368pp. 5⅜ x 8½. **T984 Paperbound $2.00**

BIRDS AND THEIR ATTRIBUTES, Glover Morrill Allen. A fine general introduction to birds as living organisms, especially valuable because of emphasis on structure, physiology, habits, behavior. Discusses relationship of bird to man, early attempts at scientific ornithology, feathers and coloration, skeletal structure including bills, legs and feet, wings. Also food habits, evolution and present distribution, feeding and nest-building, still unsolved questions of migrations and location sense, many more similar topics. Final chapter on classification, nomenclature. A good popular-level summary for the biologist; a first-rate introduction for the layman. Reprint of 1925 edition. References and index. 51 illustrations. viii + 338pp. 5⅜ x 8½. **T957 Paperbound $1.85**

LIFE HISTORIES OF NORTH AMERICAN BIRDS, Arthur Cleveland Bent. Bent's monumental series of books on North American birds, prepared and published under auspices of Smithsonian Institute, is the definitive coverage of the subject, the most-used single source of information. Now the entire set is to be made available by Dover in inexpensive editions. This encyclopedic collection of detailed, specific observations utilizes reports of hundreds of contemporary observers, writings of such naturalists as Audubon, Burroughs, William Brewster, as well as author's own extensive investigations. Contains literally everything known about life history of each bird considered: nesting, eggs, plumage, distribution and migration, voice, enemies, courtship, etc. These not over-technical works are musts for ornithologists, conservationists, amateur naturalists, anyone seriously interested in American birds.

BIRDS OF PREY. More than 100 subspecies of hawks, falcons, eagles, buzzards, condors and owls, from the common barn owl to the extinct caracara of Guadaloupe Island. 400 photographs. Two volume set. Index for each volume. Bibliographies of 403, 520 items. 197 full-page plates. Total of 907pp. 5⅜ x 8½. Vol. I **T931 Paperbound $2.50** Vol. II **T932 Paperbound $2.50**

WILD FOWL. Ducks, geese, swans, and tree ducks—73 different subspecies. Two volume set. Index for each volume. Bibliographies of 124, 144 items. 106 full-page plates. Total of 685pp. 5⅜ x 8½. Vol. I **T285 Paperbound $2.50** Vol. II **T286 Paperbound $2.50**

SHORE BIRDS. 81 varieties (sandpipers, woodcocks, plovers, snipes, phalaropes, curlews, oyster catchers, etc.). More than 200 photographs of eggs, nesting sites, adult and young of important species. Two volume set. Index for each volume. Bibliographies of 261, 188 items. 121 full-page plates. Total of 860pp. 5⅜ x 8½. Vol. I **T933 Paperbound $2.35** Vol. II **T934 Paperbound $2.35**

THE LIFE OF PASTEUR, R. Vallery-Radot. 13th edition of this definitive biography, cited in Encyclopaedia Britannica. Authoritative, scholarly, well-documented with contemporary quotes, observations; gives complete picture of Pasteur's personal life; especially thorough presentation of scientific activities with silkworms, fermentation, hydrophobia, inoculation, etc. Introduction by Sir William Osler. Index. 505pp. 5⅜ x 8. **T632 Paperbound $2.00**

Puzzles, Mathematical Recreations

SYMBOLIC LOGIC and THE GAME OF LOGIC, Lewis Carroll. "Symbolic Logic" is not concerned with modern symbolic logic, but is instead a collection of over 380 problems posed with charm and imagination, using the syllogism, and a fascinating diagrammatic method of drawing conclusions. In "The Game of Logic" Carroll's whimsical imagination devises a logical game played with 2 diagrams and counters (included) to manipulate hundreds of tricky syllogisms. The final section, "Hit or Miss" is a lagniappe of 101 additional puzzles in the delightful Carroll manner. Until this reprint edition, both of these books were rarities costing up to $15 each. Symbolic Logic: Index. xxxi + 199pp. The Game of Logic: 96pp. 2 vols. bound as one. 5⅜ x 8.   T492 Paperbound **$1.75**

PILLOW PROBLEMS and A TANGLED TALE, Lewis Carroll. One of the rarest of all Carroll's works, "Pillow Problems" contains 72 original math puzzles, all typically ingenious. Particularly fascinating are Carroll's answers which remain exactly as he thought them out, reflecting his actual mental process. The problems in "A Tangled Tale" are in story form, originally appearing as a monthly magazine serial. Carroll not only gives the solutions, but uses answers sent in by readers to discuss wrong approaches and misleading paths, and grades them for insight. Both of these books were rarities until this edition, "Pillow Problems" costing up to $25, and "A Tangled Tale" $15. Pillow Problems: Preface and Introduction by Lewis Carroll. xx + 109pp. A Tangled Tale: 6 illustrations. 152pp. Two vols. bound as one. 5⅜ x 8.   T493 Paperbound **$1.50**

AMUSEMENTS IN MATHEMATICS, Henry Ernest Dudeney. The foremost British originator of mathematical puzzles is always intriguing, witty, and paradoxical in this classic, one of the largest collections of mathematical amusements. More than 430 puzzles, problems, and paradoxes. Mazes and games, problems on number manipulation, unicursal and other route problems, puzzles on measuring, weighing, packing, age, kinship, chessboards, joiners', crossing river, plane figure dissection, and many others. Solutions. More than 450 illustrations. vii +. 258pp. 5⅜ x 8.   T473 Paperbound **$1.25**

THE CANTERBURY PUZZLES, Henry Dudeney. Chaucer's pilgrims set one another problems in story form. Also Adventures of the Puzzle Club, the Strange Escape of the King's Jester, the Monks of Riddlewell, the Squire's Christmas Puzzle Party, and others. All puzzles are original, based on dissecting plane figures, arithmetic, algebra, elementary calculus and other branches of mathematics, and purely logical ingenuity. "The limit of ingenuity and intricacy," The Observer. Over 110 puzzles. Full Solutions. 150 illustrations. vii + 225pp. 5⅜ x 8.
T474 Paperbound **$1.25**

MATHEMATICAL EXCURSIONS, H. A. Merrill. Even if you hardly remember your high school math, you'll enjoy the 90 stimulating problems contained in this book and you will come to understand a great many mathematical principles with surprisingly little effort. Many useful shortcuts and diversions not generally known are included: division by inspection, Russian peasant multiplication, memory systems for pi, building odd and even magic squares, square roots by geometry, dyadic systems, and many more. Solutions to difficult problems. 50 illustrations. 145pp. 5⅜ x 8.   T350 Paperbound **$1.00**

MAGIC SQUARES AND CUBES, W. S. Andrews. Only book-length treatment in English, a thorough non-technical description and analysis. Here are nasik, overlapping, pandiagonal, serrated squares; magic circles, cubes, spheres, rhombuses. Try your hand at 4-dimensional magical figures! Much unusual folklore and tradition included. High school algebra is sufficient. 754 diagrams and illustrations. viii + 419pp. 5⅜ x 8.   T658 Paperbound **$1.85**

CALIBAN'S PROBLEM BOOK: MATHEMATICAL, INFERENTIAL AND CRYPTOGRAPHIC PUZZLES, H. Phillips (Caliban), S. T. Shovelton, G. S. Marshall. 105 ingenious problems by the greatest living creator of puzzles based on logic and inference. Rigorous, modern, piquant; reflecting their author's unusual personality, these intermediate and advanced puzzles all involve the ability to reason clearly through complex situations; some call for mathematical knowledge, ranging from algebra to number theory. Solutions. xi + 180pp. 5⅜ x 8.
T736 Paperbound **$1.25**

MATHEMATICAL PUZZLES FOR BEGINNERS AND ENTHUSIASTS, G. Mott-Smith. 188 mathematical puzzles based on algebra, dissection of plane figures, permutations, and probability, that will test and improve your powers of inference and interpretation. The Odic Force, The Spider's Cousin, Ellipse Drawing, theory and strategy of card and board games like tit-tat-toe, go moku, salvo, and many others. 100 pages of detailed mathematical explanations. Appendix of primes, square roots, etc. 135 illustrations. 2nd revised edition. 248pp. 5⅜ x 8.
T198 Paperbound **$1.00**

MATHEMAGIC, MAGIC PUZZLES, AND GAMES WITH NUMBERS, R. V. Heath. More than 60 new puzzles and stunts based on the properties of numbers. Easy techniques for multiplying large numbers mentally, revealing hidden numbers magically, finding the date of any day in any year, and dozens more. Over 30 pages devoted to magic squares, triangles, cubes, circles, etc. Edited by J. S. Meyer. 76 illustrations. 128pp. 5⅜ x 8.   T110 Paperbound **$1.00**

THE BOOK OF MODERN PUZZLES, G. L. Kaufman. A completely new series of puzzles as fascinating as crossword and deduction puzzles but based upon different principles and techniques. Simple 2-minute teasers, word labyrinths, design and pattern puzzles, logic and observation puzzles — over 150 braincrackers. Answers to all problems. 116 illustrations. 192pp. 5⅜ x 8.
T143 Paperbound $1.00

NEW WORD PUZZLES, G. L. Kaufman. 100 ENTIRELY NEW puzzles based on words and their combinations that will delight crossword puzzle, Scrabble and Jotto fans. Chess words, based on the moves of the chess king; design-onyms, symmetrical designs made of synonyms; rhymed double-crostics; syllable sentences; addle letter anagrams; alphagrams; linkograms; and many others all brand new. Full solutions. Space to work problems. 196 figures. vi + 122pp. 5⅜ x 8.
T344 Paperbound $1.00

MAZES AND LABYRINTHS: A BOOK OF PUZZLES, W. Shepherd. Mazes, formerly associated with mystery and ritual, are still among the most intriguing of intellectual puzzles. This is a novel and different collection of 50 amusements that embody the principle of the maze: mazes in the classical tradition; 3-dimensional, ribbon, and Möbius-strip mazes; hidden messages; spatial arrangements; etc.—almost all built on amusing story situations. 84 illustrations. Essay on maze psychology. Solutions. xv + 122pp. 5⅜ x 8.
T731 Paperbound $1.00

MAGIC TRICKS & CARD TRICKS, W. Jonson. Two books bound as one. 52 tricks with cards, 37 tricks with coins, bills, eggs, smoke, ribbons, slates, etc. Details on presentation, misdirection, and routining will help you master such famous tricks as the Changing Card, Card in the Pocket, Four Aces, Coin Through the Hand, Bill in the Egg, Afghan Bands, and over 75 others. If you follow the lucid exposition and key diagrams carefully, you will finish these two books with an astonishing mastery of magic. 106 figures. 224pp. 5⅜ x 8. T909 Paperbound $1.00

PANORAMA OF MAGIC, Milbourne Christopher. A profusely illustrated history of stage magic, a unique selection of prints and engravings from the author's private collection of magic memorabilia, the largest of its kind. Apparatus, stage settings and costumes; ingenious ads distributed by the performers and satiric broadsides passed around in the streets ridiculing pompous showmen; programs; decorative souvenirs. The lively text, by one of America's foremost professional magicians, is full of anecdotes about almost legendary wizards: Dede, the Egyptian; Philadelphia, the wonder-worker; Robert-Houdin, "the father of modern magic;" Harry Houdini; scores more. Altogether a pleasure package for anyone interested in magic, stage setting and design, ethnology, psychology, or simply in unusual people. A Dover original. 295 illustrations; 8 in full color. Index. viii + 216pp. 8⅜ x 11¼.
T774 Paperbound $2.25

HOUDINI ON MAGIC, Harry Houdini. One of the greatest magicians of modern times explains his most prized secrets. How locks are picked, with illustrated picks and skeleton keys; how a girl is sawed into twins; how to walk through a brick wall — Houdini's explanations of 44 stage tricks with many diagrams. Also included is a fascinating discussion of great magicians of the past and the story of his fight against fraudulent mediums and spiritualists. Edited by W.B. Gibson and M.N. Young. Bibliography. 155 figures, photos. xv + 280pp. 5⅜ x 8.
T384 Paperbound $1.35

MATHEMATICS, MAGIC AND MYSTERY, Martin Gardner. Why do card tricks work? How do magicians perform astonishing mathematical feats? How is stage mind-reading possible? This is the first book length study explaining the application of probability, set theory, theory of numbers, topology, etc., to achieve many startling tricks. Non-technical, accurate, detailed! 115 sections discuss tricks with cards, dice, coins, knots, geometrical vanishing illusions, how a Curry square "demonstrates" that the sum of the parts may be greater than the whole, and dozens of others. No sleight of hand necessary! 135 illustrations. xii + 174pp. 5⅜ x 8.
T335 Paperbound $1.00

EASY-TO-DO ENTERTAINMENTS AND DIVERSIONS WITH COINS, CARDS, STRING, PAPER AND MATCHES, R. M. Abraham. Over 300 tricks, games and puzzles will provide young readers with absorbing fun. Sections on card games; paper-folding; tricks with coins, matches and pieces of string; games for the agile; toy-making from common household objects; mathematical recreations; and 50 miscellaneous pastimes. Anyone in charge of groups of youngsters, including hard-pressed parents, and in need of suggestions on how to keep children sensibly amused and quietly content will find this book indispensable. Clear, simple text, copious number of delightful line drawings and illustrative diagrams. Originally titled "Winter Nights Entertainments." Introduction by Lord Baden Powell. 329 illustrations. v + 186pp. 5⅜ x 8½.
T921 Paperbound $1.00

STRING FIGURES AND HOW TO MAKE THEM, Caroline Furness Jayne. 107 string figures plus variations selected from the best primitive and modern examples developed by Navajo, Apache, pygmies of Africa, Eskimo, in Europe, Australia, China, etc. The most readily understandable, easy-to-follow book in English on perennially popular recreation. Crystal-clear exposition; step-by-step diagrams. Everyone from kindergarten children to adults looking for unusual diversion will be endlessly amused. Index. Bibliography. Introduction by A. C. Haddon. 17 full-page plates. 960 illustrations. xxiii + 401pp. 5⅜ x 8½.
T152 Paperbound $2.00

Entertainments, Humor

ODDITIES AND CURIOSITIES OF WORDS AND LITERATURE, C. Bombaugh, edited by M. Gardner. The largest collection of idiosyncratic prose and poetry techniques in English, a legendary work in the curious and amusing bypaths of literary recreations and the play technique in literature—so important in modern works. Contains alphabetic poetry, acrostics, palindromes, scissors verse, centos, emblematic poetry, famous literary puns, hoaxes, notorious slips of the press, hilarious mistranslations, and much more. Revised and enlarged with modern material by Martin Gardner. 368pp. 5⅜ x 8. T759 Paperbound $1.75

A NONSENSE ANTHOLOGY, collected by Carolyn Wells. 245 of the best nonsense verses ever written, including nonsense puns, absurd arguments, mock epics and sagas, nonsense ballads, odes, "sick" verses, dog-Latin verses, French nonsense verses, songs. By Edward Lear, Lewis Carroll, Gelett Burgess, W. S. Gilbert, Hilaire Belloc, Peter Newell, Oliver Herford, etc., 83 writers in all plus over four score anonymous nonsense verses. A special section of limericks, plus famous nonsense such as Carroll's "Jabberwocky" and Lear's "The Jumblies" and much excellent verse virtually impossible to locate elsewhere. For 50 years considered the best anthology available. Index of first lines specially prepared for this edition. Introduction by Carolyn Wells. 3 indexes: Title, Author, First lines. xxxiii + 279pp. T499 Paperbound $1.35

THE BAD CHILD'S BOOK OF BEASTS, MORE BEASTS FOR WORSE CHILDREN, and A MORAL ALPHABET, H. Belloc. Hardly an anthology of humorous verse has appeared in the last 50 years without at least a couple of these famous nonsense verses. But one must see the entire volumes—with all the delightful original illustrations by Sir Basil Blackwood—to appreciate fully Belloc's charming and witty verses that play so subacidly on the platitudes of life and morals that beset his day—and ours. A great humor classic. Three books in one. Total of 157pp. 5⅜ x 8. T749 Paperbound $1.00

THE DEVIL'S DICTIONARY, Ambrose Bierce. Sardonic and irreverent barbs puncturing the pomposities and absurdities of American politics, business, religion, literature, and arts, by the country's greatest satirist in the classic tradition. Epigrammatic as Shaw, piercing as Swift, American as Mark Twain, Will Rogers, and Fred Allen, Bierce will always remain the favorite of a small coterie of enthusiasts, and of writers and speakers whom he supplies with "some of the most gorgeous witticisms of the English language" (H. L. Mencken). Over 1000 entries in alphabetical order. 144pp. 5⅜ x 8. T487 Paperbound $1.00

THE PURPLE COW AND OTHER NONSENSE, Gelett Burgess. The best of Burgess's early nonsense, selected from the first edition of the "Burgess Nonsense Book." Contains many of his most unusual and truly awe-inspiring pieces: 36 nonsense quatrains, the Poems of Patagonia, Alphabet of Famous Goops, and the other hilarious (and rare) adult nonsense that place him in the forefront of American humorists. All pieces are accompanied by the original Burgess illustrations. 123 illustrations. xiii + 113pp. 5⅜ x 8. T772 Paperbound $1.00

MY PIOUS FRIENDS AND DRUNKEN COMPANIONS and MORE PIOUS FRIENDS AND DRUNKEN COMPANIONS, Frank Shay. Folksingers, amateur and professional, and everyone who loves singing: here, available for the first time in 30 years, is this valued collection of 132 ballads, blues, vaudeville numbers, drinking songs, sea chanties, comedy songs. Songs of pre-Beatnik Bohemia; songs from all over America, England, France, Australia; the great songs of the Naughty Nineties and early twentieth-century America. Over a third with music. Woodcuts by John Held, Jr. convey perfectly the brash insouciance of an era of rollicking unabashed song. 12 illustrations by John Held, Jr. Two indexes (Titles and First lines and Choruses). Introductions by the author. Two volumes bound as one. Total of xvi + 235pp. 5⅜ x 8½. T946 Paperbound $1.25

HOW TO TELL THE BIRDS FROM THE FLOWERS, R. W. Wood. How not to confuse a carrot with a parrot, a grape with an ape, a puffin with nuffin. Delightful drawings, clever puns, absurd little poems point out far-fetched resemblances in nature. The author was a leading physicist. Introduction by Margaret Wood White. 106 illus. 60pp. 5⅜ x 8. T523 Paperbound 75¢

PECK'S BAD BOY AND HIS PA, George W. Peck. The complete edition, containing both volumes, of one of the most widely read American humor books. The endless ingenious pranks played by bad boy "Hennery" on his pa and the grocery man, the outraged pomposity of Pa, the perpetual ridiculing of middle class institutions, are as entertaining today as they were in 1883. No pale sophistications or subtleties, but rather humor vigorous, raw, earthy, imaginative, and, as folk humor often is, sadistic. This peculiarly fascinating book is also valuable to historians and students of American culture as a portrait of an age. 100 original illustrations by True Williams. Introduction by E. F. Bleiler. 347pp. 5⅜ x 8. T497 Paperbound $1.50

THE HUMOROUS VERSE OF LEWIS CARROLL. Almost every poem Carroll ever wrote, the largest collection ever published, including much never published elsewhere: 150 parodies, burlesques, riddles, ballads, acrostics, etc., with 130 original illustrations by Tenniel, Carroll, and others. "Addicts will be grateful . . . there is nothing for the faithful to do but sit down and fall to the banquet," N. Y. Times. Index to first lines. xiv + 446pp. 5⅜ x 8.
T654 Paperbound **$2.00**

DIVERSIONS AND DIGRESSIONS OF LEWIS CARROLL. A major new treasure for Carroll fans! Rare privately published humor, fantasy, puzzles, and games by Carroll at his whimsical best, with a new vein of frank satire. Includes many new mathematical amusements and recreations, among them the fragmentary Part III of "Curiosa Mathematica." Contains "The Rectory Umbrella," "The New Belfry," "The Vision of the Three T's," and much more. New 32-page supplement of rare photographs taken by Carroll. x + 375pp. 5⅜ x 8.
T732 Paperbound **$2.00**

THE COMPLETE NONSENSE OF EDWARD LEAR. This is the only complete edition of this master of gentle madness available at a popular price. A BOOK OF NONSENSE, NONSENSE SONGS, MORE NONSENSE SONGS AND STORIES in their entirety with all the old favorites that have delighted children and adults for years. The Dong With A Luminous Nose, The Jumblies, The Owl and the Pussycat, and hundreds of other bits of wonderful nonsense. 214 limericks, 3 sets of Nonsense Botany, 5 Nonsense Alphabets, 546 drawings by Lear himself, and much more. 320pp. 5⅜ x 8.
T167 Paperbound **$1.00**

THE MELANCHOLY LUTE, The Humorous Verse of Franklin P. Adams ("FPA"). The author's own selection of light verse, drawn from thirty years of FPA's column, "The Conning Tower," syndicated all over the English-speaking world. Witty, perceptive, literate, these ninety-six poems range from parodies of other poets, Millay, Longfellow, Edgar Guest, Kipling, Masefield, etc., and free and hilarious translations of Horace and other Latin poets, to satiric comments on fabled American institutions—the New York Subways, preposterous ads, suburbanites, sensational journalism, etc. They reveal with vigor and clarity the humor, integrity and restraint of a wise and gentle American satirist. Introduction by Robert Hutchinson. vi + 122pp. 5⅜ x 8½.
T108 Paperbound **$1.00**

SINGULAR TRAVELS, CAMPAIGNS, AND ADVENTURES OF BARON MUNCHAUSEN, R. E. Raspe, with 90 illustrations by Gustave Doré. The first edition in over 150 years to reestablish the deeds of the Prince of Liars exactly as Raspe first recorded them in 1785—the genuine Baron Munchausen, one of the most popular personalities in English literature. Included also are the best of the many sequels, written by other hands. Introduction on Raspe by J. Carswell. Bibliography of early editions. xliv + 192pp. 5⅜ x 8.
T698 Paperbound **$1.00**

THE WIT AND HUMOR OF OSCAR WILDE, ed. by Alvin Redman. Wilde at his most brilliant, in 1000 epigrams exposing weaknesses and hypocrisies of "civilized" society. Divided into 49 categories—sin, wealth, women, America, etc.—to aid writers, speakers. Includes excerpts from his trials, books, plays, criticism. Formerly "The Epigrams of Oscar Wilde." Introduction by Vyvyan Holland, Wilde's only living son. Introductory essay by editor. 260pp. 5⅜ x 8.
T602 Paperbound **$1.00**

MAX AND MORITZ, Wilhelm Busch. Busch is one of the great humorists of all time, as well as the father of the modern comic strip. This volume, translated by H. A. Klein and other hands, contains the perennial favorite "Max and Moritz" (translated by C. T. Brooks), Plisch and Plum, Das Rabennest, Eispeter, and seven other whimsical, sardonic, jovial, diabolical cartoon and verse stories. Lively English translations parallel the original German. This work has delighted millions since it first appeared in the 19th century, and is guaranteed to please almost anyone. Edited by H. A. Klein, with an afterword. x + 205pp. 5⅝ x 8½.
T181 Paperbound **$1.15**

HYPOCRITICAL HELENA, Wilhelm Busch. A companion volume to "Max and Moritz," with the title piece (Die Fromme Helena) and 10 other highly amusing cartoon and verse stories, all newly translated by H. A. Klein and M. C. Klein: Adventure on New Year's Eve (Abenteuer in der Neujahrsnacht), Hangover on the Morning after New Year's Eve (Der Katzenjammer am Neujahrsmorgen), etc. English and German in parallel columns. Hours of pleasure, also a fine language aid. x + 205pp. 5⅝ x 8½.
T184 Paperbound **$1.00**

THE BEAR THAT WASN'T, Frank Tashlin. What does it mean? Is it simply delightful wry humor, or a charming story of a bear who wakes up in the midst of a factory, or a satire on Big Business, or an existential cartoon-story of the human condition, or a symbolization of the struggle between conformity and the individual? New York Herald Tribune said of the first edition: ". . . a fable for grownups that will be fun for children. Sit down with the book and get your own bearings." Long an underground favorite with readers of all ages and opinions. v + 51pp. Illustrated. 5⅜ x 8½.
T939 Paperbound **75¢**

RUTHLESS RHYMES FOR HEARTLESS HOMES and MORE RUTHLESS RHYMES FOR HEARTLESS HOMES, Harry Graham ("Col. D. Streamer"). Two volumes of Little Willy and 48 other poetic disasters. A bright, new reprint of oft-quoted, never forgotten, devastating humor by a precursor of today's "sick" joke school. For connoisseurs of wicked, wacky humor and all who delight in the comedy of manners. Original drawings are a perfect complement. 61 illustrations. Index. vi + 69pp. Two vols. bound as one. 5⅜ x 8½.
T930 Paperbound **75¢**

Say It language phrase books

These handy phrase books (128 to 196 pages each) make grammatical drills unnecessary for an elementary knowledge of a spoken foreign language. Covering most matters of travel and everyday life each volume contains:

Over 1000 phrases and sentences in immediately useful forms — foreign language plus English.

Modern usage designed for Americans. Specific phrases like, "Give me small change," and "Please call a taxi."

Simplified phonetic transcription you will be able to read at sight.

The only completely indexed phrase books on the market.

Covers scores of important situations: — Greetings, restaurants, sightseeing, useful expressions, etc.

These books are prepared by native linguists who are professors at Columbia, N.Y.U., Fordham and other great universities. Use them independently or with any other book or record course. They provide a supplementary living element that most other courses lack. Individual volumes in:

Russian 75¢	Italian 75¢	Spanish 75¢	German 75¢
Hebrew 75¢	Danish 75¢	Japanese 75¢	Swedish 75¢
Dutch 75¢	Esperanto 75¢	Modern Greek 75¢	Portuguese 75¢
Norwegian 75¢	Polish 75¢	French 75¢	Yiddish 75¢
Turkish 75¢		English for German-speaking people 75¢	
English for Italian-speaking people 75¢		English for Spanish-speaking people 75¢	

Large clear type. 128-196 pages each. 3½ x 5¼. Sturdy paper binding.

Listen and Learn language records

LISTEN & LEARN is the only language record course designed especially to meet your travel and everyday needs. It is available in separate sets for FRENCH, SPANISH, GERMAN, JAPANESE, RUSSIAN, MODERN GREEK, PORTUGUESE, ITALIAN and HEBREW, and each set contains three 33⅓ rpm long-playing records—1½ hours of recorded speech by eminent native speakers who are professors at Columbia, New York University, Queens College.

Check the following special features found only in LISTEN & LEARN:

● **Dual-language recording.** 812 selected phrases and sentences, over 3200 words, spoken first in English, then in their foreign language equivalents. A suitable pause follows each foreign phrase, allowing you time to repeat the expression. You learn by unconscious assimilation.

● **128 to 206-page manual** contains everything on the records, plus a simple phonetic pronunciation guide.

● **Indexed for convenience. The only set on the market** that is completely indexed. No more puzzling over where to find the phrase you need. Just look in the rear of the manual.

● **Practical.** No time wasted on material you can find in any grammar. LISTEN & LEARN covers central core material with phrase approach. Ideal for the person with limited learning time.

● **Living, modern expressions,** not found in other courses. Hygienic products, modern equipment, shopping—expressions used every day, like "nylon" and "air-conditioned."

● **Limited objective.** Everything you learn, no matter where you stop, is immediately useful. You have to finish other courses, wade through grammar and vocabulary drill, before they help you.

● **High-fidelity recording.** LISTEN & LEARN records equal in clarity and surface-silence any record on the market costing up to $6.

"Excellent . . . the spoken records . . . impress me as being among the very best on the market," **Prof. Mario Pei,** Dept. of Romance Languages, Columbia University. "Inexpensive and well-done . . . it would make an ideal present," CHICAGO SUNDAY TRIBUNE. "More genuinely helpful than anything of its kind which I have previously encountered," **Sidney Clark,** well-known author of "ALL THE BEST" travel books.

UNCONDITIONAL GUARANTEE. Try LISTEN & LEARN, then return it within 10 days for full refund if you are not satisfied.

Each set contains three twelve-inch 33⅓ records, manual, and album.

SPANISH	the set $5.95	GERMAN	the set $5.95
FRENCH	the set $5.95	ITALIAN	the set $5.95
RUSSIAN	the set $5.95	JAPANESE	the set $6.95
PORTUGUESE	the set $5.95	MODERN GREEK	the set $5.95
MODERN HEBREW	the set $5.95		

Americana

THE EYES OF DISCOVERY, J. Bakeless. A vivid reconstruction of how unspoiled America appeared to the first white men. Authentic and enlightening accounts of Hudson's landing in New York, Coronado's trek through the Southwest; scores of explorers, settlers, trappers, soldiers. America's pristine flora, fauna, and Indians in every region and state in fresh and unusual new aspects. "A fascinating view of what the land was like before the first highway went through," Time. 68 contemporary illustrations, 39 newly added in this edition. Index. Bibliography. x + 500pp. 5⅜ x 8. T761 Paperbound $2.25

AUDUBON AND HIS JOURNALS, J. J. Audubon. A collection of fascinating accounts of Europe and America in the early 1800's through Audubon's own eyes. Includes the Missouri River Journals —an eventful trip through America's untouched heartland, the Labrador Journals, the European Journals, the famous "Episodes", and other rare Audubon material, including the descriptive chapters from the original letterpress edition of the "Ornithological Studies", omitted in all later editions. Indispensable for ornithologists, naturalists, and all lovers of Americana and adventure. 70-page biography by Audubon's granddaughter. 38 illustrations. Index. Total of 1106pp. 5⅜ x 8.
T675 Vol I Paperbound $2.25
T676 Vol II Paperbound $2.25
The set $4.50

TRAVELS OF WILLIAM BARTRAM, edited by Mark Van Doren. The first inexpensive illustrated edition of one of the 18th century's most delightful books is an excellent source of first-hand material on American geography, anthropology, and natural history. Many descriptions of early Indian tribes are our only source of information on them prior to the infiltration of the white man. "The mind of a scientist with the soul of a poet," John Livingston Lowes. 13 original illustrations and maps. Edited with an introduction by Mark Van Doren. 448pp. 5⅜ x 8.
T13 Paperbound $2.00

GARRETS AND PRETENDERS: A HISTORY OF BOHEMIANISM IN AMERICA, A. Parry. The colorful and fantastic history of American Bohemianism from Poe to Kerouac. This is the only complete record of hoboes, cranks, starving poets, and suicides. Here are Pfaff, Whitman, Crane, Bierce, Pound, and many others. New chapters by the author and by H. T. Moore bring this thorough and well-documented history down to the Beatniks. "An excellent account," N. Y. Times. Scores of cartoons, drawings, and caricatures. Bibliography. Index. xxviii + 421pp. 5⅝ x 8⅜. T708 Paperbound $1.95

THE EXPLORATION OF THE COLORADO RIVER AND ITS CANYONS, J. W. Powell. The thrilling first-hand account of the expedition that filled in the last white space on the map of the United States. Rapids, famine, hostile Indians, and mutiny are among the perils encountered as the unknown Colorado Valley reveals its secrets. This is the only uncut version of Major Powell's classic of exploration that has been printed in the last 60 years. Includes later reflections and subsequent expedition. 250 illustrations, new map. 400pp. 5⅝ x 8⅜.
T94 Paperbound $2.25

THE JOURNAL OF HENRY D. THOREAU, Edited by Bradford Torrey and Francis H. Allen. Henry Thoreau is not only one of the most important figures in American literature and social thought; his voluminous journals (from which his books emerged as selections and crystallizations) constitute both the longest, most sensitive record of personal internal development and a most penetrating description of a historical moment in American culture. This present set, which was first issued in fourteen volumes, contains Thoreau's entire journals from 1837 to 1862, with the exception of the lost years which were found only recently. We are reissuing it, complete and unabridged, with a new introduction by Walter Harding, Secretary of the Thoreau Society. Fourteen volumes reissued in two volumes. Foreword by Henry Seidel Canby. Total of 1888pp. 8⅜ x 12¼. T312-3 Two volume set, Clothbound $20.00

GAMES AND SONGS OF AMERICAN CHILDREN, collected by William Wells Newell. A remarkable collection of 190 games with songs that accompany many of them; cross references to show similarities, differences among them; variations; musical notation for 38 songs. Textual discussions show relations with folk-drama and other aspects of folk tradition. Grouped into categories for ready comparative study: Love-games, histories, playing at work, human life, bird and beast, mythology, guessing-games, etc. New introduction covers relations of songs and dances to timeless heritage of folklore, biographical sketch of Newell, other pertinent data. A good source of inspiration for those in charge of groups of children and a valuable reference for anthropologists, sociologists, psychiatrists. Introduction by Carl Withers. New indexes of first lines, games. 5⅜ x 8½. xii + 242pp. T354 Paperbound $1.75

Art, History of Art, Antiques, Graphic Arts, Handcrafts

ART STUDENTS' ANATOMY, E. J. Farris. Outstanding art anatomy that uses chiefly living objects for its illustrations. 71 photos of undraped men, women, children are accompanied by carefully labeled matching sketches to illustrate the skeletal system, articulations and movements, bony landmarks, the muscular system, skin, fasciae, fat, etc. 9 x-ray photos show movement of joints. Undraped models are shown in such actions as serving in tennis, drawing a bow in archery, playing football, dancing, preparing to spring and to dive. Also discussed and illustrated are proportions, age and sex differences, the anatomy of the smile, etc. 8 plates by the great early 18th century anatomic illustrator Siegfried Albinus are also included. Glossary. 158 figures, 7 in color. x + 159pp. 5⅝ x 8⅜. T744 Paperbound **$1.50**

AN ATLAS OF ANATOMY FOR ARTISTS, F Schider. A new 3rd edition of this standard text enlarged by 52 new illustrations of hands, anatomical studies by Cloquet, and expressive life studies of the body by Barcsay. 189 clear, detailed plates offer you precise information of impeccable accuracy. 29 plates show all aspects of the skeleton, with closeups of special areas, while 54 full-page plates, mostly in two colors, give human musculature as seen from four different points of view, with cutaways for important portions of the body. 14 full-page plates provide photographs of hand forms, eyelids, female breasts, and indicate the location of muscles upon models. 59 additional plates show how great artists of the past utilized human anatomy. They reproduce sketches and finished work by such artists as Michelangelo, Leonardo da Vinci, Goya, and 15 others. This is a lifetime reference work which will be one of the most important books in any artist's library. "The standard reference tool," AMERICAN LIBRARY ASSOCIATION. "Excellent," AMERICAN ARTIST. Third enlarged edition. 189 plates, 647 illustrations. xxvi + 192pp. 7⅞ x 10⅝. T241 Clothbound **$6.00**

AN ATLAS OF ANIMAL ANATOMY FOR ARTISTS, W. Ellenberger, H. Baum, H. Dittrich. The largest, richest animal anatomy for artists available in English. 99 detailed anatomical plates of such animals as the horse, dog, cat, lion, deer, seal, kangaroo, flying squirrel, cow, bull, goat, monkey, hare, and bat. Surface features are clearly indicated, while progressive beneath-the-skin pictures show musculature, tendons, and bone structure. Rest and action are exhibited in terms of musculature and skeletal structure and detailed cross-sections are given for heads and important features. The animals chosen are representative of specific families so that a study of these anatomies will provide knowledge of hundreds of related species. "Highly recommended as one of the very few books on the subject worthy of being used as an authoritative guide," DESIGN. "Gives a fundamental knowledge," AMERICAN ARTIST. Second revised, enlarged edition with new plates from Cuvier, Stubbs, etc. 288 illustrations. 153pp. 11⅜ x 9. T82 Clothbound **$6.00**

THE HUMAN FIGURE IN MOTION, Eadweard Muybridge. The largest selection in print of Muybridge's famous high-speed action photos of the human figure in motion. 4789 photographs illustrate 162 different actions: men, women, children—mostly undraped—are shown walking, running, carrying various objects, sitting, lying down, climbing, throwing, arising, and performing over 150 other actions. Some actions are shown in as many as 150 photographs each. All in all there are more than 500 action strips in this enormous volume, series shots taken at shutter speeds of as high as 1/6000th of a second! These are not posed shots, but true stopped motion. They show bone and muscle in situations that the human eye is not fast enough to capture. Earlier, smaller editions of these prints have brought $40 and more on the out-of-print market. "A must for artists," ART IN FOCUS. "An unparalleled dictionary of action for all artists," AMERICAN ARTIST. 390 full-page plates, with 4789 photographs. Printed on heavy glossy stock. Reinforced binding with headbands. xxi + 390pp. 7⅞ x 10⅝. T204 Clothbound **$10.00**

ANIMALS IN MOTION, Eadweard Muybridge. This is the largest collection of animal action photos in print. 34 different animals (horses, mules, oxen, goats, camels, pigs, cats, guanacos, lions, gnus, deer, monkeys, eagles—and 21 others) in 132 characteristic actions. The horse alone is shown in more than 40 different actions. All 3919 photographs are taken in series at speeds up to 1/6000th of a second. The secrets of leg motion, spinal patterns, head movements, strains and contortions shown nowhere else are captured. You will see exactly how a lion sets his foot down; how an elephant's knees are like a human's—and how they differ; the position of a kangaroo's legs in mid-leap; how an ostrich's head bobs; details of the flight of birds—and thousands of facets of motion only the fastest cameras can catch. Photographed from domestic animals and animals in the Philadelphia zoo, it contains neither semiposed artificial shots nor distorted telephoto shots taken under adverse conditions. Artists, biologists, decorators, cartoonists, will find this book indispensable for understanding animals in motion. "A really marvelous series of plates," NATURE (London). "The dry plate's most spectacular early use was by Eadweard Muybridge," LIFE. 3919 photographs; 380 full pages of plates. 440pp. Printed on heavy glossy paper. Deluxe binding with headbands. 7⅞ x 10⅝. T203 Clothbound **$10.00**

THE AUTOBIOGRAPHY OF AN IDEA, Louis Sullivan. The pioneer architect whom Frank Lloyd Wright called "the master" reveals an acute sensitivity to social forces and values in this passionately honest account. He records the crystallization of his opinions and theories, the growth of his organic theory of architecture that still influences American designers and architects, contemporary ideas, etc. This volume contains the first appearance of 34 full-page plates of his finest architecture. Unabridged reissue of 1924 edition. New introduction by R. M. Line. Index. xiv + 335pp. 5⅜ x 8. **T281 Paperbound $2.00**

THE DRAWINGS OF HEINRICH KLEY. The first uncut republication of both of Kley's devastating sketchbooks, which first appeared in pre-World War I Germany. One of the greatest cartoonists and social satirists of modern times, his exuberant and iconoclastic fantasy and his extraordinary technique place him in the great tradition of Bosch, Breughel, and Goya, while his subject matter has all the immediacy and tension of our century. 200 drawings. viii + 128pp. 7¾ x 10¾. **T24 Paperbound $1.85**

MORE DRAWINGS BY HEINRICH KLEY. All the sketches from Leut' Und Viecher (1912) and Sammel-Album (1923) not included in the previous Dover edition of Drawings. More of the bizarre, mercilessly iconoclastic sketches that shocked and amused on their original publication. Nothing was too sacred, no one too eminent for satirization by this imaginative, individual and accomplished master cartoonist. A total of 158 illustrations. Iv + 104pp. 7¾ x 10¾. **T41 Paperbound $1.85**

PINE FURNITURE OF EARLY NEW ENGLAND, R. H. Kettell. A rich understanding of one of America's most original folk arts that collectors of antiques, interior decorators, craftsmen, woodworkers, and everyone interested in American history and art will find fascinating and immensely useful. 413 illustrations of more than 300 chairs, benches, racks, beds, cupboards, mirrors, shelves, tables, and other furniture will show all the simple beauty and character of early New England furniture. 55 detailed drawings carefully analyze outstanding pieces. "With its rich store of illustrations, this book emphasizes the individuality and varied design of early American pine furniture. It should be welcomed," ANTIQUES. 413 illustrations and 55 working drawings. 475. 8 x 10¾. **T145 Clothbound $10.00**

THE HUMAN FIGURE, J. H. Vanderpoel. Every important artistic element of the human figure is pointed out in minutely detailed word descriptions in this classic text and illustrated as well in 430 pencil and charcoal drawings. Thus the text of this book directs your attention to all the characteristic features and subtle differences of the male and female (adults, children, and aged persons), as though a master artist were telling you what to look for at each stage. 2nd edition, revised and enlarged by George Bridgman. Foreword. 430 illustrations. 143pp. 6⅛ x 9¼. **T432 Paperbound $1.50**

LETTERING AND ALPHABETS, J. A. Cavanagh. This unabridged reissue of LETTERING offers a full discussion, analysis, illustration of 89 basic hand lettering styles — styles derived from Caslons, Bodonis, Garamonds, Gothic, Black Letter, Oriental, and many others. Upper and lower cases, numerals and common signs pictured. Hundreds of technical hints on make-up, construction, artistic validity, strokes, pens, brushes, white areas, etc. May be reproduced without permission! 89 complete alphabets; 72 lettered specimens. 121pp. 9⅜ x 8. **T53 Paperbound $1.35**

STICKS AND STONES, Lewis Mumford. A survey of the forces that have conditioned American architecture and altered its forms. The author discusses the medieval tradition in early New England villages; the Renaissance influence which developed with the rise of the merchant class; the classical influence of Jefferson's time; the "Mechanicsvilles" of Poe's generation; the Brown Decades; the philosophy of the Imperial facade; and finally the modern machine age. "A truly remarkable book," SAT. REV. OF LITERATURE. 2nd revised edition. 21 illustrations. xvii + 228pp. 5⅜ x 8. **T202 Paperbound $1.75**

THE STANDARD BOOK OF QUILT MAKING AND COLLECTING, Marguerite Ickis. A complete easy-to-follow guide with all the information you need to make beautiful, useful quilts. How to plan, design, cut, sew, appliqué, avoid sewing problems, use rag bag, make borders, tuft, every other aspect. Over 100 traditional quilts shown, including over 40 full-size patterns. At-home hobby for fun, profit. Index. 483 illus. 1 color plate. 287pp. 6¾ x 9½. **T582 Paperbound $2.00**

THE BOOK OF SIGNS, Rudolf Koch. Formerly $20 to $25 on the out-of-print market, now only $1.00 in this unabridged new edition! 493 symbols from ancient manuscripts, medieval cathedrals, coins, catacombs, pottery, etc. Crosses, monograms of Roman emperors, astrological, chemical, botanical, runes, housemarks, and 7 other categories. Invaluable for handicraft workers, illustrators, scholars, etc., this material may be reproduced without permission. 493 illustrations by Fritz Kredel. 104pp. 6½ x 9¼. **T162 Paperbound $1.00**

PRIMITIVE ART, Franz Boas. This authoritative and exhaustive work by a great American anthropologist covers the entire gamut of primitive art. Pottery, leatherwork, metal work, stone work, wood, basketry, are treated in detail. Theories of primitive art, historical depth in art history, technical virtuosity, unconscious levels of patterning, symbolism, styles, literature, music, dance, etc. A must book for the interested layman, the anthropologist, artist, handicrafter (hundreds of unusual motifs), and the historian. Over 900 illustrations (50 ceramic vessels, 12 totem poles, etc.). 376pp. 5⅜ x 8. **T25 Paperbound $2.25**

Fiction

FLATLAND, E. A. Abbott. A science-fiction classic of life in a 2-dimensional world that is also a first-rate introduction to such aspects of modern science as relativity and hyperspace. Political, moral, satirical, and humorous overtones have made FLATLAND fascinating reading for thousands. 7th edition. New introduction by Banesh Hoffmann. 16 illustrations. 128pp. 5⅜ x 8.
T1 Paperbound **$1.00**

THE WONDERFUL WIZARD OF OZ, L. F. Baum. Only edition in print with all the original W. W. Denslow illustrations in full color—as much a part of "The Wizard" as Tenniel's drawings are of "Alice in Wonderland." "The Wizard" is still America's best-loved fairy tale, in which, as the author expresses it, "The wonderment and joy are retained and the heartaches and nightmares left out." Now today's young readers can enjoy every word and wonderful picture of the original book. New introduction by Martin Gardner. A Baum bibliography. 23 full-page color plates. viii + 268pp. 5⅜ x 8.
T691 Paperbound **$1.50**

THE MARVELOUS LAND OF OZ, L. F. Baum. This is the equally enchanting sequel to the "Wizard," continuing the adventures of the Scarecrow and the Tin Woodman. The hero this time is a little boy named Tip, and all the delightful Oz magic is still present. This is the Oz book with the Animated Saw-Horse, the Woggle-Bug, and Jack Pumpkinhead. All the original John R. Neill illustrations, 10 in full color. 287 pp. 5⅜ x 8.
T692 Paperbound **$1.50**

28 SCIENCE FICTION STORIES OF H. G. WELLS. Two full unabridged novels, MEN LIKE GODS and STAR BEGOTTEN, plus 26 short stories by the master science-fiction writer of all time! Stories of space, time, invention, exploration, future adventure—an indispensable part of the library of everyone interested in science and adventure. PARTIAL CONTENTS: Men Like Gods, The Country of the Blind, In the Abyss, The Crystal Egg, The Man Who Could Work Miracles, A Story of the Days to Come, The Valley of Spiders, and 21 more! 928pp. 5⅜ x 8.
T265 Clothbound **$4.50**

THREE MARTIAN NOVELS, Edgar Rice Burroughs. Contains: Thuvia, Maid of Mars; The Chessmen of Mars; and The Master Mind of Mars. High adventure set in an imaginative and intricate conception of the Red Planet. Mars is peopled with an intelligent, heroic human race which lives in densely populated cities with fierce barbarians who inhabit dead sea bottoms. Other exciting creatures abound amidst an inventive framework of Martian history and geography. Complete unabridged reprintings of the first edition. 16 illustrations by J. Allen St. John. vi + 499pp. 5⅜ x 8½.
T39 Paperbound **$1.85**

SEVEN SCIENCE FICTION NOVELS, H. G. Wells. Full unabridged texts of 7 science-fiction novels of the master. Ranging from biology, physics, chemistry, astronomy to sociology and other studies, Mr. Wells extrapolates whole worlds of strange and intriguing character. "One will have to go far to match this for entertainment, excitement, and sheer pleasure . . . ," NEW YORK TIMES. Contents: The Time Machine, The Island of Dr. Moreau, First Men in the Moon, The Invisible Man, The War of the Worlds, The Food of the Gods, In the Days of the Comet. 1015pp. 5⅜ x 8.
T264 Clothbound **$4.50**

THE LAND THAT TIME FORGOT and THE MOON MAID, Edgar Rice Burroughs. In the opinion of many, Burroughs' best work. The first concerns a strange island where evolution is individual rather than phylogenetic. Speechless anthropoids develop into intelligent human beings within a single generation. The second projects the reader far into the future and describes the first voyage to the Moon (in the year 2025), the conquest of the Earth by the Moon, and years of violence and adventure as the enslaved Earthmen try to regain possession of their planet. "An imaginative tour de force that keeps the reader keyed up and expectant," NEW YORK TIMES. Complete, unabridged text of the original two novels (three parts in each). 5 illustrations by J. Allen St. John. vi + 552pp. 5⅜ x 8½.
T1020 Clothbound **$3.75**
T358 Paperbound **$2.00**

3 ADVENTURE NOVELS by H. Rider Haggard. Complete texts of "She," "King Solomon's Mines," "Allan Quatermain." Qualities of discovery; desire for immortality; search for primitive, for what is unadorned by civilization, have kept these novels of African adventure exciting, alive to readers from R. L. Stevenson to George Orwell. 636pp. 5⅜ x 8.
T584 Paperbound **$2.00**

A PRINCESS OF MARS and A FIGHTING MAN OF MARS: TWO MARTIAN NOVELS BY EDGAR RICE BURROUGHS. "Princess of Mars" is the very first of the great Martian novels written by Burroughs, and it is probably the best of them all; it set the pattern for all of his later fantasy novels and contains a thrilling cast of strange peoples and creatures and the formula of Olympian heroism amidst ever-fluctuating fortunes which Burroughs carries off so successfully. "Fighting Man" returns to the same scenes and cities—many years later. A mad scientist, a degenerate dictator, and an indomitable defender of the right clash—with the fate of the Red Planet at stake! Complete, unabridged reprinting of original editions. Illustrations by F. E. Schoonover and Hugh Hutton. v + 356pp. 5⅜ x 8½.
T1140 Paperbound **$1.75**

Music

A GENERAL HISTORY OF MUSIC, Charles Burney. A detailed coverage of music from the Greeks up to 1789, with full information on all types of music: sacred and secular, vocal and instrumental, operatic and symphonic. Theory, notation, forms, instruments, innovators, composers, performers, typical and important works, and much more in an easy, entertaining style. Burney covered much of Europe and spoke with hundreds of authorities and composers so that this work is more than a compilation of records . . . it is a living work of careful and first-hand scholarship. Its account of thoroughbass (18th century) Italian music is probably still the best introduction on the subject. A recent NEW YORK TIMES review said, "Surprisingly few of Burney's statements have been invalidated by modern research . . . still of great value." Edited and corrected by Frank Mercer. 35 figures. Indices. 1915pp. 5⅜ x 8. 2 volumes. **T36 The Set, Clothbound $12.50**

A DICTIONARY OF HYMNOLOGY, John Julian. This exhaustive and scholarly work has become known as an invaluable source of hundreds of thousands of important and often difficult to obtain facts on the history and use of hymns in the western world. Everyone interested in hymns will be fascinated by the accounts of famous hymns and hymn writers and amazed by the amount of practical information he will find. More than 30,000 entries on individual hymns, giving authorship, date and circumstances of composition, publication, textual variations, translations, denominational and ritual usage, etc. Biographies of more than 9,000 hymn writers, and essays on important topics such as Christmas carols and children's hymns, and much other unusual and valuable information. A 200 page double-columned index of first lines — the largest in print. Total of 1786 pages in two reinforced clothbound volumes. 6¼ x 9¼. **The set, T333 Clothbound $17.50**

MUSIC IN MEDIEVAL BRITAIN, F. Ll. Harrison. The most thorough, up-to-date, and accurate treatment of the subject ever published, beautifully illustrated. Complete account of institutions and choirs; carols, masses, and motets; liturgy and plainsong; and polyphonic music from the Norman Conquest to the Reformation. Discusses the various schools of music and their reciprocal influences; the origin and development of new ritual forms; development and use of instruments; and new evidence on many problems of the period. Reproductions of scores, over 200 excerpts from medieval melodies. Rules of harmony and dissonance; influence of Continental styles; great composers (Dunstable, Cornysh, Fairfax, etc.); and much more. Register and index of more than 400 musicians. Index of titles. General Index. 225-item bibliography. 6 Appendices. xix + 491pp. 5⅝ x 8¾. **T705 Clothbound $10.00**

THE MUSIC OF SPAIN, Gilbert Chase. Only book in English to give concise, comprehensive account of Iberian music; new Chapter covers music since 1941. Victoria, Albéniz, Cabezón, Pedrell, Turina, hundreds of other composers; popular and folk music; the Gypsies; the guitar; dance, theatre, opera, with only extensive discussion in English of the Zarzuela; virtuosi such as Casals; much more. "Distinguished . . . readable," Saturday Review. 400-item bibliography. Index. 27 photos. 383pp. 5⅜ x 8. **T549 Paperbound $2.25**

ON STUDYING SINGING, Sergius Kagen. An intelligent method of voice-training, which leads you around pitfalls that waste your time, money, and effort. Exposes rigid, mechanical systems, baseless theories, deleterious exercises. "Logical, clear, convincing . . . dead right," Virgil Thomson, N.Y. Herald Tribune. "I recommend this volume highly," Maggie Teyte, Saturday Review. 119pp. 5⅜ x 8. **T622 Paperbound $1.35**

Prices subject to change without notice.

Dover publishes books on art, music, philosophy, literature, languages, history, social sciences, psychology, handcrafts, orientalia, puzzles and entertainments, chess, pets and gardens, books explaining science, intermediate and higher mathematics, mathematical physics, engineering, biological sciences, earth sciences, classics of science, etc. Write to:

Dept. catrr.
Dover Publications, Inc.
180 Varick Street, N.Y. 14, N.Y.